VISITORS' HISTORIC BRITAIN

SOMERSET

STONE AGE TO WWII

VISITORS' HISTORIC BRITAIN

SOMERSET

STONE AGE TO WWII

MICK DAVIS & DAVID LASSMAN

PEN & SWORD
HISTORY

AN IMPRINT OF PEN & SWORD BOOKS LTD
YORKSHIRE - PHILADELPHIA

First published in Great Britain in 2020 by
Pen & Sword History
An imprint of
Pen & Sword Books Ltd
Yorkshire – Philadelphia

ISBN 978 1 52670 616 4

A CIP catalogue record for this book is
available from the British Library.

Printed and bound in England
By TJ International Ltd, Padstow, Cornwall
Typeset by Aura Technology and Software Services, India.

Pen & Sword Books Limited incorporates the imprints of Atlas, Archaeology, Aviation, Discovery, Family History, Fiction, History, Maritime, Military, Military Classics, Politics, Select, Transport, True Crime, Air World, Frontline Publishing, Leo Cooper, Remember When, Seaforth Publishing, The Praetorian Press, Wharncliffe Local History, Wharncliffe Transport, Wharncliffe True Crime and White Owl.

For a complete list of Pen & Sword titles please contact

PEN & SWORD BOOKS LIMITED
47 Church Street, Barnsley, South Yorkshire, S70 2AS, England
E-mail: enquiries@pen-and-sword.co.uk
Website: www.pen-and-sword.co.uk

Or
PEN AND SWORD BOOKS
1950 Lawrence Rd, Havertown, PA 19083, USA
E-mail: Uspen-and-sword@casematepublishers.com
Website: www.penandswordbooks.com

*To Bish, whose love of history is only surpassed by his love of cider,
and to Axel F & Neil E, as I would never be able to live it down if
I did not include them as well – DL*

To Lorraine who has helped more than she knows – MD

Contents

Acknowledgements

The maps included here are from the excellent OpenStreetMap.org site which are available to all and are intended as a guide only; for more detailed information the relevant Ordnance Survey maps should be consulted.

Graphics are taken in the main from the equally excellent Geograph.org.uk site and individual photographers duly credited, others are either from our own collections or are credited beneath the caption.

Much historical information has been obtained from numerous guidebooks and county guides too numerous to list.

Most pub details are taken from the incredibly informative CAMRA site WhatPub.com and a goodly few from personal investigation, but it must be stressed that details are subject to change at any time and should always be checked before making a visit. Some pubs stop selling food in the afternoons, whilst others follow the quaint old English habit of closing completely during this time. Phone first to avoid disappointment!

A huge thank you is also due to our publishers Pen & Sword, and in particular to Heather Williams whose patience we tried on more than one occasion when pleading for 'just a little more time'.

Introduction

Welcome to the Visitor's Historic Britain for Somerset. Every inch of this legendary county is steeped in history, from the towns of Dunster and Taunton in the west, to those of Shepton Mallet and Frome in the east; while also contained within the county boundaries are the great cities of Bath and Wells, and the mystical and magical Isle of Avalon: Glastonbury.

Somerset has been inhabited as far back as the Palaeolithic, or Old Stone Age, which is, in fact, the period of the earliest known occupation of Britain by humans. These include archaeological sites such as Cheddar Gorge and Gough's Cave – which has been dated to 12000 BC – while a complete skeleton, known as Cheddar Man (Chapter 3), is dated to 7150 BC and the oldest cemetery – dated to around 10,000 years ago, was discovered at Aveline's Hole (Chapter 7). At the same time, one of the world's oldest known engineered roadways – the Sweet Track (Chapter 5) – can be found within the county. In terms of Neolithic sites, Stonehenge and Avebury may be across the border in Wiltshire, but Somerset can claim its own megalith, in the Stanton Drew Stone Circle (Chapter 7). It is the second largest stone circle (after Avebury) in Britain and is, in fact, considered to be one of the largest Neolithic monuments to have been built. It is thought to have been constructed in the late Neolithic to the Early Bronze Age, roughly between 3000 and 2000 BC. As for Hill Forts, the county is literally dotted with them. Most can be dated to the Iron Age and include among the most well-known, Cow Castle (Chapter 1), Norton Camp & Kings Castle (Chapter 2), Brent Knoll (Chapter 3) Cadbury Castle (Chapter 4) Maesbury Castle (Chapter 5), Little Solsbury Hill (Chapter 6) and Cadbury Camp (Chapter 7).

It is not just the man-made landmarks that make the county so interesting, in terms of historical heritage. Raw materials have played a huge part in defining the county's past. The Romans made a direct beeline for the lead (and silver) in the mines at Mendip, after they had invaded Britain in AD 43. Lead was essential for the smooth running of the Roman Empire; as it was a key element in piping, plumbing, pewter, coffins and gutters for villas. Because of this, mining became one of the most prosperous activities in Roman Britain. Fifty-two sheets of Mendip lead apparently line the great bath at Bath (Chapter 6) and research has supposedly also shown that Somerset lead was used in Pompeii – the town destroyed in the eruption of Vesuvius in AD 79. Other than the mines in the Mendips, most notably at Charterhouse, Roman Somerset can boast numerous villas, the spa complex at Bath (Chapter 6), a large part of the Roman road, the Fosse Way, and the Frome Hoard, one of the largest finds of Roman coins in the country (Chapter 4).

After the Roman withdrawal at the beginning of the fifth century, Somerset later became part of the legendary ancient kingdom of Wessex which at one time was led by King Alfred the Great. The site of the 'burnt cakes' incident is said to have occurred within the Somerset Levels, while Alfred was in hiding, and it was also in the county, at Athelney, Alfred made his base from which he launched the resistance movement against the Danes that culminated in the victory at Edington in 878.

In the Middle Ages, wool became big business; indeed, the raw material became the backbone and driving force of the medieval English economy for two centuries from the late thirteenth onwards. Many towns in Somerset became major centres for the wool trade and became very prosperous through it; for some places, in Frome (Chapter 5) for example, it became the principal industry, with the manor of Frome eventually passing into the ownership of a cloth merchant near the beginning of the eighteenth century.

Although Somerset's contribution to the English Civil War was perhaps not as significant as other counties, the siege of Dunster (Chapter 1) and the Battle of Lansdown (Chapter 6) perhaps the exceptions, it is probably fair to say that the Monmouth Rebellion became, for all accounts, a Somerset phenomenon. Apart from a couple of early skirmishes around Lyme Regis and nearby Axminister, not long after the Duke of Monmouth had landed at the former, the entire Monmouth Rebellion, Revolt of the West, West Country Rebellion, Pitchfork Rebellion, whatever you wish to call it, took place within the county's boundaries; from Monmouth's declaration of kingship at Chard and Taunton (Chapter 2) through rebel victories such as Norton St Philip (Chapter 5) to Monmouth's eventual defeat at the Battle of Sedgemoor (Chapter 3) and the king's bloody retribution, in the form of the Assizes (Chapter 3).

Along with wool, and cider making – the county's contribution to the world's alcoholic drinks cabinet – numerous cottage industries (businesses and crafts carried on within their owner's cottages, hence the name) sprang up throughout the county over the centuries, but when the industrial revolution took hold in the Midlands and Northern England, it spelled the end for most of them. The workers did not go quietly though, as there were many incidents of industrial damage to machinery and rioting. Farming continued to flourish, however, and coal mining became a major industry in the county.

Although known as the Somerset Coalfield, the mining of coal only took place at certain locations in the north of the county, mainly within the Mendip Hills; in an area that encompassed Nettlebridge and Coleford in the southern tip of the coalfield, up to around Pensford (Chapter 7), with Nailsea and Bath being the west and east markers, respectively. The coalfield was, in fact, part of a larger coalfield that stretched up into southern Gloucestershire (as far as the village of Cromhall). Coal in Somerset was mined from the fifteenth century until the 1970s. Most of the pits within the coalfield were concentrated in the Cam Brook, Wellow Brook and Nettlebridge Valleys and around Radstock (Chapter 6) and Farrington Gurney. The pits were grouped geographically, with clusters of pits close together working the same coal seams, often under the same ownership. The coal was then transported either by railway or on the Somerset Coal Canal. The deepest shaft on the coalfield was at the Strap mine at Nettlebridge, which reached almost 2,000ft. There is still evidence of mine workings, with the remains of buildings, spoil heaps and tramways in the area, but to fully understand the history of coal mining in the area, a visit to the Radstock Museum (Chapter 6) is highly recommended.

War was always a factor in historical Somerset, whether it was localised (The Monmouth Rebellion), national (English Civil War) or else global (First and Second World War) the men and women of the county rose to the occasion. In terms of military heritage, the county, like many others, had its own regiment associated with itself. The Somerset Light Infantry began life in 1685 as one of nine regiments of foot raised by James II, in response to the Monmouth Rebellion. As the Earl of Huntingdon was authorised to raise the regiment it was subsequently called, unsurprisingly, the Earl of Huntingdon's Regiment of Foot. It went through a series of minor name changes during the following century, until 1782, when its association with Somerset began. With the belief that county-named regiments would increase recruitment within those relevant counties, the 13th (1st Somersetshire) Regiment of Foot came into being in August 1782. This later incorporated the title Prince Albert's Light Infantry, after the prince offered his patronage, following the regiment's conduct at Jalalabad in 1841. By the time of the First World War, the regiment had become simply Prince Albert's (Somerset Light Infantry) Regiment, and before World War Two, changed a final time to The Somerset Light Infantry (Prince Albert's). In 1959, the regiment amalgamated with the Duke of Cornwall's Light Infantry. At this time, the regiment could look back on its history with pride, having undertaken engagements within numerous conflicts, including the Nine Years War, the war of 1812, the Second Boer War, both world wars and the Suez Crisis. For a history of the regiment, along with other units associated with the county – such as the West and North Yeomanry and the Somerset Militia – visit the Somerset Military Museum in Taunton (Chapter 2).

During the First World War many men from Somerset died in the trenches of France and Flanders and elsewhere, and the county's regiment itself suffered nearly 5,000 casualties. There were, however, nine 'Thankful Villages' in Somerset, more than any other county. This term – coined in the 1930s – was used to describe a village that lost none of its men in the Great War. The villages are Aisholt, Chantry, Chelwood, Holywell Lake (a hamlet in Thorne St Margaret), Rodney Stoke, Shapwick, Stocklinch, Tellisford and Woolley. In fact, two of these are what is known as 'Doubly Thankful Villages', as neither Stocklinch or Woolley lost any of its men in the Second World War, either.

Somerset became a reception area early in the Second World War, which meant it took many thousands of evacuated children from bomb-threatened areas, mainly around London. The county then became one long defensive line, with the construction of the Taunton Stop Line (and to a lesser extent the Yellow one) – a series of obstacles, both man-made and natural – assembled to repel any German invasion of Britain. After this did not materialise, the county became a regular target for German bombers, and this included the infamous Bath Blitz (Chapter 6). Later in the war, the county also became a marshalling area for the build-up of American, and other, troops, before they moved south to the disembarkation areas to launch the invasion of Normandy in June 1944, otherwise known as the D-Day landings. Reminders of the war can be seen at places throughout the county, although the various museums dedicated to its history are perhaps a good first stop.

Somerset has been divided into seven sections, based mainly upon the administrative divisions which exists in the county at this time. The sections are Exmoor, Taunton Deane, Sedgemoor, South Somerset, Mendip, Bath and North East Somerset, and North Somerset. Within each of these sections the authors have attempted to highlight all points of historical interest in a circuitous route, although it is left to the readers to either follow our lead, or else to select a completely different approach to the various sites. Whatever route you take and whatever sites you choose to visit, we hope this guide will be informative and be a springboard from which to dive deep into Somerset's rich and illustrious heritage.

We have excluded for the most part, opening times, prices and other details that can swiftly go out of date (often between writing them and the publication of the book!). This decision has been reinforced by the ease at which information – up to date and accurate – can be obtained from the internet (www.visitsomerset.co.uk) and most, if not all, visitors have easy access to it. With this in mind, we have aimed to give a more cohesive narrative to the text, giving enough detail to enjoy your visit, but at the same time, hopefully as a foundation to learning more about the sites and wider context surrounding them. We also hope the book could be read in the comfort of your armchair and that you would still be transported to the places mentioned, as if you had travelled there under your own steam. Having said that, however, if one did merely travel by 'armchair', a whole aspect of experience would be sadly missed, as one cannot mention Somerset without mentioning its landscape. Although this book is historical in nature, most of the county's epoch-making activity has been played out against a backdrop of dramatic and breath-taking beauty, from vast tracts of land such as Exmoor, hill ranges such as Mendip and Blackdown and an abundance of incredible rivers, lakes and streams, many situated within the famous Somerset Levels.

Whichever way you choose to travel into the legendary county of Somerset and whatever use you make of this Visitor's Historic Guide to Somerset, we hope that the book will serve to provide readers with information in the reading, but also with enjoyment, entertainment and fun in the doing.

Mick Davis and David Lassman June 2019

CHAPTER 1

West Somerset

We begin our journey into **West Somerset** at County Gate, where this part of Somerset meets Devon. The largely rural area has a population of around 35,000, spread out over an area of nearly 300 square miles making it the least populous non-unitary district in England. This sense of space and expansiveness is immediately evident as the border is located within **Exmoor National Park** (www.exmoor-nationalpark.gov. uk) which strides both counties. Exmoor was designated a National Park in 1954 and at one time was a royal forest and hunting ground. It has been said that of:

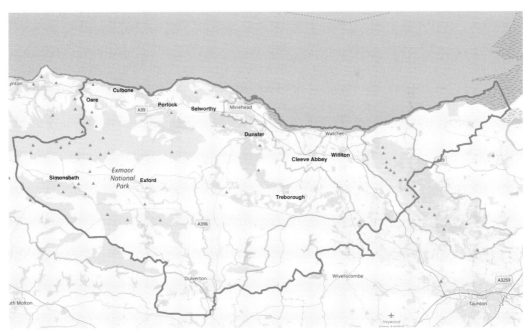

Map of West Somerset.

all the National Parks of England and Wales, Exmoor has the greatest range of natural scenery. While it has none of the rugged grandeur of the mountains of Snowdonia or the Lake District, the bleak upland moors of Dartmoor or such an extent or range of sea cliff as the Pembrokeshire Coastal Park, Exmoor has a little of all of them and a bit more besides.

As breath-taking as this region can be in terms of natural beauty, this is predominately an historical guidebook and so the main points of interest here will be the man-made 'footprints' which mark out this landscape. Very often though, this historical legacy and nature's presence blend into one, creating a fascinating place to explore.

Travelling on the A39 eastwards from County Gate, the tiny hamlet of **Oare** is soon signposted. Recorded in the Domesday book as Are, it is a later association that entices most visitors to this area. For this is **Doone Country** (www.visit-exmoor.co.uk/experience/doone-country) now forever associated with R.D. Blackmore's most famous and popular novel *Lorna Doone*, which chronicles the love affair between the title character and local farmer John Ridd. As Blackmore was a frequent visitor during his childhood, it is perhaps not surprising that he used this landscape as a backdrop for his novel, and the author did confess that he had allowed himself considerable licence and that, 'If I had dreamed that it would ever be more than a book of the moment, 'the descriptions of scenery – which I know as well as I know my garden – would have been kept nearer to their fact.' Despite this, there is still plenty to allow lovers of the novel, first published in 1869, to fully immerse themselves in this seventeenth-century tale of romance, murder and revenge. Among the 'landmarks' to be seen are **Lorna Doone Farm** (the setting for Nicholas Snowe's farm in the book), **Oare House**, supposedly the model for John Ridd's Plover's Barrow Farm, **Robber's Bridge** – where Ridd's father was murdered – and **Badgworthy Water** (which in the book is slightly amended to Bagworthy). There is also a memorial stone to the author, placed in 1969, which commemorates the publication's centenary.

Of note is **Oare church**, where Blackmore's grandfather was at one time rector and Lorna was shot on her wedding day by Carver Doone;

the window through which the offending bullet was fired being dutifully marked. The church too has a memorial to the author. It seems to be firmly established that the story on which the novel was based is essentially true, although the author moved the events forward twenty years, in order to incorporate the Monmouth Rebellion within his narrative.

Leaving one literary association behind, and travelling eastward once more, a village is soon approached that has another, later connection. Although its bay is now silted, it seems more than likely **Porlock** (www.porlock.co.uk) was once a major port. The Vikings launched a raid at the start of the tenth century but were beaten back by the local inhabitants, while to add to the invaders' woes, their ships were wrecked on nearby Steep Holm. Even worse was to follow as, stuck on the small island, they ultimately lost their lives through starvation. More than a century later, in 1052, a Saxon army did successfully land there. For a history of this coastal village, along with a collection of photographs of the infamous **Porlock Hill**, visit the **Doverhay Manor Museum**) (www.doverymanormuseum. org.uk) which is also known as the Porlock Museum and is housed in the late fifteenth-century Manor House, situated in the High Street. The **Boat Shed Museum** at 3 Highbank, Porlock, is a small museum begun by Derek Purvis, fisherman, photographer and local historian which provides visitors with a varied collection of artefacts and information that will enhance the experience of this historic port.

An event from the final year of the nineteenth century though is probably the most famous maritime tale associated with this area. The **Great Porlock Rescue** occurred throughout the night of 12/13 January 1899. On that date the *Forest Hall* – a 1,900-ton, three-mast ship – found itself in difficulties while navigating the waters around Porlock and the alarm was raised for the Lynmouth lifeboat, the *Louisa*, to be launched. The crew were unable to set out from their home port, due to the atrocious weather, and so it was decided to take the boat over land and launch it at Porlock's more sheltered harbour. Twenty horses and 100 men undertook the perilous journey of fifteen miles, which saw the widening of several sections of roads, the demolition of a garden wall and felling of a large tree, not to mention the several miles of wild Exmoor paths the ten-ton lifeboat and carriage had to traverse across. Once all that was achieved, the rescue party then had to descend the steep and treacherous **Porlock Hill** before the end of their gruelling overland endeavour. Incredibly, they reached their destination at 6.30 in the morning and launched the lifeboat. Despite being hungry, cold, saturated and exhausted, they then rowed for more than an hour in stormy seas to rescue all eighteen crew members of the *Forest Hall* with no loss of human life (although apparently four horses died through their earlier exertion).

Although this feat of human endurance and fortitude was immortalised in a children's historical novel seventy years after the event, this is not the literary association for which the village is famous. Although Samuel Taylor Coleridge and William Wordsworth are universally known as 'Lake Poets' (through their association with the Lake District) and are largely responsible for the instigation of the Romantic movement in poetry, the county of Somerset played an equally important part in the development of their reputation as two of the greatest poets England has ever produced. Coleridge first met Wordsworth in 1795 and within two years both were living in Somerset; Coleridge with his family at a cottage in Nether Stowey, Wordsworth with his sister, Dorothy, at Alfoxton House (Chapter 3).

During the time they spent in the county, they produced the first edition of 'Lyrical Ballads', a collaboration between them which included such poems as Wordsworth's famous 'Tintern Abbey' and Coleridge's 'The Rime of the Ancient Mariner'. In 1797, a century before the Great Porlock Rescue, the poet Samuel Taylor Coleridge (www.exmoor-nationalpark.gov. uk/Whats-Special/culture/literary-links/samuel-taylor-coleridge) rented a cottage in the village of **Culbone** – a two-mile walk from the picturesque small harbour of **Porlock Weir** – to try and cure the ill-health he had been experiencing for some while (Coleridge was at the time living on the Quantocks). It was at this cottage, legend has it, that he awoke from a drug-fuelled sleep and with the book he had been reading earlier on Mongol leader Kublai Khan – grandson of the famous Genghis Khan – as his inspiration, began to transcribe the poem which had appeared fully formed in his head on waking. He was only a mere fifty-four lines in, on what would have been a several-hundred-line epic, when there was a knock on the cottage door. The visitor's name and purpose have been lost but we know where they came from, as they have forever become known as the 'Person from Porlock'. Whatever the trivial matter was, it occupied enough of the increasingly frustrated poet's time to render the remaining lines of the poem, once he was alone again, lost to posterity. The exact site of the cottage where Coleridge wrote *Kubla Khan* is disputed, but the now-demolished **Withycombe Farm** is the favoured choice of most experts, although nearby **Ash Farm** is a close second. In terms of residencies, there are at least two further 'Coleridge Cottages' named as such elsewhere in Somerset. One is in Nether Stowey at 35 Lime Street, while the other is at Clevedon (Chapter 7) where he stayed for his honeymoon in 1795.

On the beach at Porlock Weir there are a couple of pillboxes from the Second World War which are worth exploring. They are faced with large pebbles, which helps them to blend in well, but having been built on a beach they are slowly subsiding.

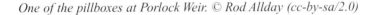

One of the pillboxes at Porlock Weir. © Rod Allday (cc-by-sa/2.0)

Nearby is **Culbone Church** (www.minehead-online.co.uk/culbone.
htm) which is officially the smallest parish church in England. Although
its date of construction is unknown, this Grade I listed building is
believed to be Saxon. It doubled as Oare church in a television version
of *Lorna Doone* and featured in Mike and the Mechanics' 1988 video of
the hit song *The Living Years*. In the fourteenth century the surrounding
woods housed a prison colony for French soldiers – as it did again in the
eighteenth. There was also another colony established within Culbone's
steep wooded landscape – a leper colony – whose inhabitants were reputed
to be burners for the charcoal burning industry sited in the area at one
time. To add weight to this, there is a small leper window in the north wall
of the church.

Of further interest is the **Culbone Stone,** an early mediaeval standing
stone approximately a metre in height and dated to somewhere between
the seventh and ninth century. It lies in woodland close to the parish

The tiny church of Culbone. © Philip Halling (cc-by-sa/2.0)

boundary, between Porlock and Oare, and features an incised wheeled cross – a Christian symbol. It was discovered recumbent during the early years of the Second World War and placed upright in its present position but is believed to have originally formed part of the nearby **Culbone Hill Stone Row**. The stone has been scheduled as an ancient monument and although on private land, can be viewed by the public via a permissive pathway.

Still carrying along the A39 and making a left-turn, we come to **Selworthy** (www.nationaltrust.org.uk/selworthy). Although appearing in the Domesday Book, where it was recorded as Selewrda, it was rebuilt as a 'model village' in 1828 by Sir Thomas Acland – in a similar style to Blaise Hamlet, Bristol, a few years earlier – to provide housing for the aged and infirm of the Holnicote estate. It is now in the hands of the National Trust, having been given to them in 1944. Although very few buildings on the estate survive from before 1828, those that do include the church, tithe barn and Tithe Barn Cottage.

Located nearby, and part of Selworthy parish, is the village of **Allerford** and its much-photographed **Packhorse Bridge.** One of the village's main attractions, the bridge was originally built as a crossing over the River Aller (from where the village derives its name) and is believed to date from medieval times. The bridge has been deemed an ancient monument and has been added to the 'Heritage at Risk' register. Interestingly, a much later construction, the **Allerford New Bridge**, is also on the 'risk' register because of constant vehicle damage and general erosion. The **Allerford Museum** is situated within the old village school. The museum includes the Victorian school room and the West Somerset Photographic Archive. The school, built in 1821, was in use until 1981 before becoming the Rural Life Museum. It is self-supporting and all members of staff are volunteers. Meanwhile, **Bury Castle**, a nearby Iron Age hill fort, can be reached by a walk through the surrounding woods.

The next main port of call, following the A39, is the coastal town of **Minehead** (www.visitsomerset.co.uk/explore-somerset/minehead) located on the south bank of the Bristol Channel. Although possibly best known for being this part of Somerset's chief holiday resort, which includes a Butlin's holiday camp that has resided here since the 1960s, this port had its heyday, in historical terms, much earlier. Although like elsewhere in West Somerset there is evidence of Iron and Bronze age occupation, it was during the fourteenth century through to the mid-eighteenth century that the harbour developed into a major trading centre; its importance being especially recognised during the English Civil War when it was fiercely fought over by Parliamentarian and Royalist forces. A few years earlier, privateers involved in the war with Spain and France based themselves here, as they did again during the War of the Spanish Succession at the beginning of the eighteenth century. A fire in 1791 destroyed many buildings in the middle and lower towns, but after rebuilding, the resort reinvented itself as a place for sea bathing.

Another form of transport which has played a major role in Minehead's history is the railway. **Minehead Railway Station** first opened in 1874 as the terminus of the Minehead Railway, but was closed by British Rail in 1971. It reopened five years later and is now headquarters of the **West Somerset Railway** (www.west-somerset-railway.co.uk). **Minehead Museum** (www.mineheadmuseum.co.uk) located in Beeches Hotel, lies opposite Minehead railway station and entry is through the Information Centre at the hotel. Exhibits show the fascinating history of Minehead, including the Hobby Horse (see below), The Great Fire, the life of world-famous author, Sir Arthur C. Clarke, and the pier which was dismantled in the 1940s.

One popular and ancient Minehead tradition involves the **Hobby Horse**, (www.minehead-online.co.uk/hobbyhorse.htm) which makes its appearance on the eve of 1 May each year, accompanied by musicians and rival horses, and cavorts about for the following four days. The three rival horses are known as the Original Sailor's Horse, the Traditional Sailor's Horse and the Town Horse. They appear on May Eve, known as 'Show Night', while on May Day morning they salute the sunrise at a crossroads on the outskirts of town. The evenings of the next two days witness a ceremony called 'The Bootie', which takes place in the part of town called Cher. Each horse is made of a boat-shaped wooden frame, pointed and built up at each end, which is carried on the dancer's shoulders. Its resemblance to any known breed of horse is slight to say the least.

The Hobby Horse in around 1900. (Museum of Somerset).

A vivid description of this tradition was recorded in 1830:

A number of young men, mostly fishermen and sailors, having previously made some grotesque figures of light stuff, rudely resembling men, and horses with long tails, sufficiently large to cover and disguise the persons who are to carry them, assemble together and perambulate the town and neighbourhood, performing a variety of antics, to the great amusement of the children and young persons. They never fail to pay a visit to Dunster Castle, where, after having been hospitably regaled with strong beer and victuals, they always receive a present in money; many other persons, inhabitants of the places they visit, give them small sums, and such persons as they meet are also asked to contribute a trifle; if they are refused, the person of the refuser is subjected to the ceremony of booting or pursing; this is done by some of the attendants holding his person while one of the figures inflict ten slight blows on him with the top of a boot; he is then liberated and all parties give three huzzas: the most trifling sum buys off this ceremony, and it is seldom or never performed but on those who purposely throw themselves in their way and join the party, or obstruct them in their vagaries. This custom has prevailed for ages, but what gave rise to it is at present unknown: it probably owes its origin to some ancient custom of perambulating the boundaries of the parish.

Money collected from these 'Bootie Nights' are given to various charities, including the Royal National Lifeboat Institution (RNLI).

The medieval village of nearby **Dunster** (www.dunster.org.uk) still within the boundary of Exmoor National Park is, as one writer has recorded, 'a real gem'. Although Iron Age hillforts testify to the area's occupation during past millennia and there was also a Saxon frontier post at one time. The present-day village came into existence after the Norman Conquest in 1066. For most of its history, the Lords of the Manor were the Luttrell family. It became a centre of the wool trade and one reminder of this period exists in the form of the **Yarn Market** (www.english-heritage.org.uk/visit/places/dunster-yarn-market/) an octagonal structure around a central pier and located within the High Street. Built in the early

The Gallox Bridge Dunster. © Richard Croft (cc-by-sa/2.0)

seventeenth century, it is today designated a Grade I listed building. Other points of historical interest include the still working **Dunster Water Mill**, which grinds flour for local bakeries, and the **Gallox Bridge**, a medieval packhorse bridge; its name apparently a corruption of gallows, after one that stood on a nearby hill.

The main attraction for most visitors will probably be **Dunster Castle** (www.nationaltrust.org.uk/dunster-castle) around which the village grew. The local historian R.W. Dunning has written that 'the view of Dunster Castle from the distance is almost fairytale', and no doubt few visitors would disagree. But although this was the purpose of Anthony Salvin's reconstruction for the Luttrell family in the mid-nineteenth century, it belies the fact that at its core is a military stronghold of Norman origin, set atop an almost impregnable clifftop. And these elements have served it well during the many times of conflict it has experienced in its more than 1,000-year history. Built sometime between 1066 and 1086, by William de Mohun, it was defended by a later namesake against King Stephen during the civil war of the Anarchy period – when it was a stronghold of the rival for the crown, Empress Matilda – and was in the thick of the action again during the later English Civil War, in the seventeenth century.

Initially a Parliamentarian garrison at the start of the hostilities, in 1642, its then owner Thomas Luttrell changed sides the following year, yielding to Sir Francis Wyndham, despite having withstood a Royalist siege. It reverted to the side of the eventual victors in 1646, after another siege – this one lasting six months – and was then held until the end of the civil war. Although near starvation – the cause of its surrender during the later siege – the castle's occupants nevertheless found the strength and energy to march out of the castle with honour. The Victorian era reconstruction in the 1870s turned the castle into a splendid country house of the period, although it retained its fine seventeenth century carved staircase and ornate plaster ceilings, while a century later, it passed into the hands of the National Trust. Evidence of its former 'life' surfaced during its remodelling in the shape of a skeleton of a male, manacled, walled up and left to die, discovered in one of the gatehouse towers, known to have been used a dungeon.

English Civil War

The English Civil War – comprising a series of armed conflicts – took place between 1642 and 1651 and was primarily a clash over the governance of England. On one side stood the Royalists (Cavaliers), who favoured the continued rule of the monarch – who at the time was King Charles I – while on the other were the Parliamentarians (Roundheads) who wanted to abolish the monarchy and have the country ruled as a republic. Ultimately the Parliamentarians were victorious, and this led to the execution of Charles I, the exile of his son, the later Charles II, and the replacement of the monarchy by first the Commonwealth of England and then what was known as the Protectorate, initially under the leadership of Oliver Cromwell. This civil war, as most do, divided families, friends and neighbours and saw many parts of the country suffer massive destruction and huge loss of life.

Somerset, along with neighbouring counties of Gloucestershire and Wiltshire, became of great importance to both armies during this conflict. This was due to the supply of food, uniforms and munitions the area was able to give, the control of vital transport routes in it – either by road or river – and the fact that in each county lay a major port; in Somerset's case this was Minehead. Not surprisingly, then, the county was fiercely fought over and during the nine years of conflict, it witnessed battles, sieges and much bloodshed.

At the beginning of hostilities North Somerset, with its ports and clothing towns, was primarily sympathetic to the Parliamentarian cause, with the rest of the county being either neutral or moderately Royalist. Due to the reasons explained, both the king and parliament quickly dispatched forces to try and gain control of Somerset; and by the end of 1642 it was in the hands of the latter. The following year, however, with the arrival of Ralph Hopton's new Royalist army sweeping into the county from Cornwall, the balance of power briefly shifted, and military garrisons was established at Dunster (Chapter 1), Taunton (Chapter 2) and Bridgwater (Chapter 3).

To counteract this, Parliament despatched further forces into Somerset, under the auspices of Sir William Waller and it was therefore only a matter of time before the two armies met in open conflict; which took place at Lansdown, just outside Bath (see chapter 6). The battle was inconclusive although the Royalist forces suffered grave losses. A few days later the defeat of Parliament at Devizes enabled a Royalist victory at Bath. With the county now truly in Royalist hands, a network of further garrisons was established in places such as Berkeley, Fairleigh and Nunney (Chapter 5).

This changed again when Parliamentarians captured Taunton in 1644, which led to a prolonged siege later that year and another in the following year (Chapter 2). 1645 also saw the arrival of the New Model Army and with it, parliament was able to reclaim Somerset once and for all, although not without the spilling of much blood and another devastating siege (this time at Bridgwater). Outside of the county, the decisive parliamentary victories at the Battles of Naseby and Langport effectively destroyed the armies of King Charles I, and led to his capture in early 1646. What has become known as the First English Civil War was over; although there would be a second and third phase, Somerset played little part in these.

Of further interest is the **Conygar Tower**, which lies to the north-west of the village on an opposite hillside to the castle. Commissioned in 1775 by Henry Luttrell, and designed by Richard Phelps, this three-storey, circular Grade II listed building was no more than a grand folly, being created solely as a landmark. One legend has it that the tower and castle are linked by a subterranean passageway, but as one observer has stated, if so, then 'it is a very long tunnel.' Another place to visit is the Memorial Hall in the High Street, which houses the **Dunster Museum & Doll Collection** (www. dunstermuseum.co.uk) with over 800 dolls from around the world.

The village of **Carhampton,** near Dunster, contains the remains of **Bat's Castle.** This is an Iron Age hillfort with two stone ramparts and the same number of ditches, located at the top of a 700ft hill. It was only discovered in recent times but may once have been the legendary fortress of Din Draithou and associated with the famous Irish king and raider, Crimthann mac Fidaig. Lying seven miles to the south of Dunster is the small village of **Treborough**, sited among the Brendon Hills within the Exmoor National Park, its attractions include an unusual pair of lime kilns which date from the early nineteenth century and are made from flat-bedded local slate.

Like many other places in West Somerset, the delightful town of **Dulverton** (www.visitsomerset.co.uk/explore-somerset/dulverton) was once an important centre of the wool trade and is surrounded by Iron Age hillforts; in this case the 'castles' of **Oldberry**, **Mounsey** and **Brewers**. Nearby, and of further historic interest, is **Tarr Steps** (www.exmoor-nationalpark.gov.uk/enjoying/tarr-steps) located seven miles north-west of the town and nestled in the deeply wooded Barle valley. This is a clapper bridge that spans the River Barle and stands within a national nature reserve, itself inside the boundary of Exmoor National Park. It is of a typical construction for this sort of bridge and is more than likely of medieval origin, although it has also been associated with the much earlier Iron Age Celts. Either way, it is now a Grade I listed building and Scheduled Ancient Monument. A local story goes that the Devil built the bridge at Tarr Steps and still has sunbathing rights on its stones. The myth says that the devil swore he would kill anyone who tried to cross his bridge. The terrified locals got the parson to face him. A cat was sent over the bridge but was vaporised in a puff of smoke. The parson then set off and met the Devil midway. The Devil swore and intimidated him, but the parson reciprocated and finally the Devil agreed to let people pass except when he wants to sunbathe, so visitors are asked to take special care on sunny days. Whoever placed them there, their handiwork has been no match for the forces of nature which have, at various times since its creation, swept many of the stones away; most spectacularly in 1952, when the floods that devastated Lynmouth, across the border in Devon, washed sixteen of the seventeen spans away, including one slab weighing more than a ton, which was moved nearly 50m (164ft) downstream! More recently, in December 2012, when half the bridge was swept away but rebuilt, and again in November 2016. Another place to visit nearby is the **Guildhall Heritage and Arts Centre** (www.dulvertonheritagecentre.org.uk) and exhibitions include the local archives, an audio-visual display about Dulverton and its surroundings. The working model railway with its detailed reconstruction of the original Dulverton Station is a very popular exhibit.

Hillforts

Hillforts developed in Britain during the Late Bronze and Early Iron Age, roughly the start of the first millennium BC. The reason for their emergence and purpose has been a subject of much debate and they probably served a variety of uses; defensive military sites constructed in response to threatened invasion from the continent, a reaction to tribal tensions at home, tribal gathering places, as well as expressions of wealth and power. One view is that their construction was stimulated by the change from the production of bronze to iron and the resulting tensions arising from this due to the change in the location of raw materials. Much more archaeological investigation is needed to solve the problem. What is not in doubt is their vast size. Many are huge, with the largest being Maiden Castle in Dorset, enclosing an incredible 47 acres. There are numerous sites throughout Somerset; the most famous being **Cadbury Castle** (Chapter 4) located five miles north east of Yeovil, which shows definite signs of conflict during the time of Roman invasion – as well as later occupation by Romans and Saxons. Other notable hillforts worth seeing within the county include **Cow Castle** (Chapter 1), **Norton Camp & Kings Castle** (Chapter 2), **Brent Knoll** (Chapter 3) **Maesbury Castle** (Chapter 5) and **Cadbury Camp** (Chapter 7).

Around the coast from the town of Minehead is the small port of **Watchet** (www.visit-watchet.co.uk). The town has a history dating back over 1,000 years, during which time its harbour was in regular competition for trade with neighbouring ones. **The Market House Museum** (watchetmuseum. co.uk) located in a two-storey stone building in Market Street is a good place to learn about the port's history, as well as viewing fossils excavated from surrounding hills, while **Watchet Boat Museum** (www.somersetmuseums. co.uk/2018/12/12/watchet-boat-museum/) in Harbour Road, celebrates the history of the flatner boats. This type of maritime vessel, flat bottomed with no keel, is local to this area and were used on the mud flats, once the tide had gone out. The building in which the museum is housed began life as a goods shed and terminus for the Bristol and Exeter Railway and was designed by Brunel.

Cleeve Abbey Gatehouse © Ken Grainger (cc-by-sa/2.0)

Daw's Castle (also known as Dart's Castle or Dane's Castle) is a hill fort west of Watchet, named after Thomas Dawe who owned **Castell Field** in the early sixteenth century. The fortification may be of Iron Age origin but was (re)built and fortified by King Alfred, as part of his chain of coastal defence against Viking raids from the Bristol Channel around the late ninth century.

Inland from Watchet is **Williton** (www.visitsomerset.co.uk/explore-somerset/williton), which is the administrative centre for West Somerset. Sights of historical interest include **Orchard Wyndham**, a Grade I listed manor house, parts of which are medieval; **The Giant's Cave,** a grotto situated within its grounds; and the neighbouring Grade II listed **Bailiff's House.** Also close by is **Nettlecombe Court**, an estate on the northern fringes of the Brendon Hills but within Exmoor National Park. This sixteenth-century Grade I listed building contains Elizabethan, Tudor and medieval architecture, along with Georgian refinements. It is set within a 150-acre park, which itself is listed Grade II on the National Register of Historic Parks and Gardens. **The Bakelite Museum** (www. bakelitemuseum.net/) is housed in Orchard Mill, and includes vintage plastics such as radios, cameras, telephones, Bayko play bricks and a Bakelite car, vintage caravans and even a Bakelite coffin. An additional feature is the contents of one of the first, pioneering Bakelite factories in Britain, with presses, moulding machines and over 120 steel moulds (at the time of writing, however, there is a notice on the museum's website to say that it is now closed for relocation, and to 'Watch this space!' for future news about the new site).

Within the same area can be found **Cleeve Abbey** (www.english-heritage.org.uk/visit/places/cleeve-abbey). This Cistercian building is said to be 'one of the jewels of Somerset' and to contain the finest cloister buildings in the whole of England giving a glimpse of monastic life 800 years ago; although the abbey church was destroyed by Henry VIII during the dissolution in 1536, the cloister buildings, including the gatehouse, fifteenth-century refectory with its glorious angel roof, and thirteenth-century heraldic tiles have survived remarkably intact.

Elsewhere within West Somerset is the delightful village of **Simonsbath**, (www.exmoor-nationalpark.gov.uk/learning/the-moorland-classroom/

simonsbath) high up in the Exmoor hills and which has the distinction of being not only the largest civil parish on Exmoor, but also the most sparsely populated with only 156 people at the last census.

Nearby is the **Exmoor Forest Inn** (www.exmoorforestinn.co.uk) reputedly the haunt of noted Exmoor highwayman Tom Faggus, along with his trusty strawberry mare, Winnie. Several traps were set to catch him, but he seems to have escaped all except the final one. There is no record of his execution, but whatever happened to him in real life, he lives on in fiction, having been immortalised by R.D. Blackmore in *Lorna Doone*. Also, within this locale is **Cow Castle**, an Iron Age hill fort about four miles south west of Exford. It occupies an isolated hilltop with a single rampart and ditch. If local legend is believed, the hillfort was built by fairies for their protection.

We now leave West Somerset and head south-east, towards the Taunton Deane area; one steeped in rebel blood and historical significance in terms of monarchy.

Food and Drink

Queen's Head Inn, Holloway Street Minehead TA24 5NR 01643 702 940

In a side street just off the Parade, this popular town pub sells up to eight ales including a house beer 'Queens Head' which is very reasonably priced. There is an extensive food menu offering English and Thai food as well as a Wednesday and Sunday carvery. The spacious single bar has a raised seating area for dining and families. The pub features a skittle alley and games room at the back. Live music is a feature on a Saturday.

Bottom Ship Inn Porlock Weir TA24 8PB 01643 862 507 enquiries@shipinnporlock.co.uk

This ancient pub is situated in the picturesque location of Porlock Weir, a 15th Century hamlet overlooking the Bristol Channel. The harbour is an old fishing weir and is now a popular destination with small ships and boats. There are several shops in keeping with the attractive surroundings and a small aquarium attraction nearby. The pub offers five bed and breakfast rooms all ensuite, real ale and folk singers (sometimes).

The Railway Inn 55 Long Street, Williton, TA4 4QY 01984 632508

The Railway Inn is also known as the Foresters Arms and is a popular local. Very busy during the summer months because of its proximity to the West Somerset Railway. The large garden at the back is very popular then. There is also live music in the summer. Various activities throughout the year like pool, darts, skittles and quizzes. A guest beer is available during the busier season.

The Star Inn Mill Lane Watchet TA23 OBZ 01984 631 367

A friendly Freehouse and real ale pub with a welcoming bar, log fire and good food to go with good beer. In the summer the large beer garden is open and well behaved dogs on a lead are welcome throughout the pub. The pub was first documented as the Royal Oak in 1794 and the first landlord was Josiah Watts 1794 – 1808. Robert Stoate closed and reopened the pub during 1825 as the Star Inn. During its history the pub was owned by the Egremont trustees in the 1870's then the Wyndham Estate in the 1890's. Situated next to a babbling brook and you can always hear the sea from the pub. Exmoor beef & duck. CAMRA Pub of the Year 2006

Peeples Tavern 24 Market St, Watchet TA23 0AN 01984 634 737

Over 30 ciders & as many beers Winners of the CAMRA Somerset Cider Pub of the Year from 2014-2018 music evenings – no food but fish & chips may be brought in from next door or orders can be rung through to the local deli.

The Butchers Arms. Main Road, Carhampton TA24 6LP 01643 821333

About 4 miles west of Minehead along the A39, this pub has the date 1638 made from knucklebones and set into the floor of the bar., and is one of the few remaining pubs to continue the ancient tradition of 'wassailing' which gathers small groups of people who go house-visiting from door to door to sing and offer a drink from a wassail bowl of cider. The event takes place in the orchard behind the pub on January 17 the old 'Twelfth Night' from the Julian calendar. Bed & Breakfast available

The Stags Head Inn 10 West St, Dunster TA24 6SN 01643 821229
info@stagsheadinnexmoor

A 5-minute walk from the 17th-century Yarn Market, this traditional
16th-century inn set in Exmoor National Park is a 6-minute walk from
Dunster Castle and 2.3 miles from the West Somerset Railway. Rooms
featuring country-style decor have TVs, and tea and coffeemaking
facilities, plus paid Wi-Fi access. Cooked breakfast is included and
one room features a fresco dating back to the Reformation. There's
restaurant with a bar, stone walls and a fireplace serving a pub classics
and a beer garden. Guidebooks can be borrowed from the bar.

CHAPTER 2

Taunton Deane

Historical landmarks pepper the area and from here, there are two choices. One is to go back onto the B3188 and complete the journey to the Anglo-Saxon settlement of Wiveliscombe, or to the east lies **King's Castle**, another ancient hillfort with two banks around it and a ditch between them. Arrowheads, scrapers, and borers have been found at the site along with hoard of 1,139 coins found in a pot buried 1ft below the surface.

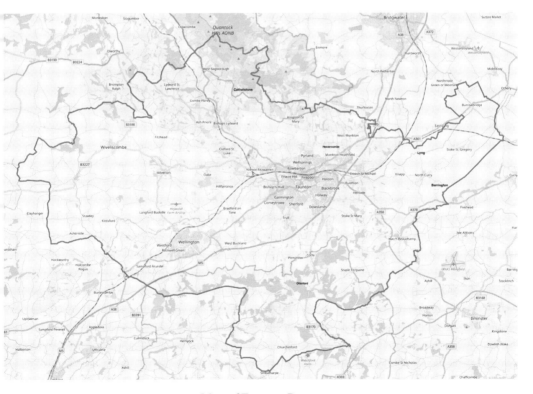

Map of Taunton Deane.

Unfortunately, the site has been heavily damaged by repeated quarrying and ploughing. Three miles to the north-west of the town is **Clatworthy Camp**, an Iron Age hillfort and scheduled ancient monument which has been added to the Heritage at Risk register due to its vulnerability to scrub and tree growth. Although the site's history is unclear, it seems to have been used during the Bronze and Iron Ages and is situated on a promontory of the Brendon Hills, above Clatworthy reservoir. The fort is roughly triangular with a single bank and ditch cut through solid rock. There may have been an entrance on the western side, with two others on the east. The interior has a series of postholes, which suggests either a timber or stone structure. On the other side of Wiveliscombe, south of nearby Manor Farm and near the village of Bathealton, is the remains of what is known locally as 'The Castle', but which was identified as a **Roman Fort** back in the eighteenth century. It was during this period that a hoard of 1,600 Roman coins, dated to the third and fourth centuries, was discovered.

The second route, is to carry on from Tolland and connect again with the B3224. Carry on along this road for a little while in the direction of Taunton, and about six miles to the northwest of the town, turn off for the village of Combe Florey. The English writer, wit and Anglican cleric, Sydney Smith, was rector here for many years during the nineteenth century, while **Combe Florey House** was once the home of novelist Evelyn Waugh, and later of his son, Auberon, who is buried in St Peter and St Paul's churchyard. Evelyn Waugh is buried in a private plot of land next to the churchyard. Daisy and Alexander Waugh, both writers, also grew up in the house.

From here, we reach the A358 and head once more in the direction of Taunton. About five miles to the north-west of the town lies the village of **Bishops Lydeard** (www.visitsomerset.co.uk/explore-somerset/bishops-lydeard) with a population of 2,839 people in the 2011 census (if you include the village of Cotford St Luke). For a small village there is plenty to see. The **Bishops Lydeard Railway Station** (www.west-somerset-railway.co.uk/railway/stations/bishops-lydeard) lies appropriately enough in Station Road and is a 'heritage' railway with many exhibits. On the original platform is the restored goods shed and this is used as both visitor's centre and museum; its artefacts include a Great Western Railway sleeping car, while the Taunton

Model Railway Club's model railway layout is on display. The village is also the southern terminus for the West Somerset Railway, a privately owned line that runs for almost twenty miles to Minehead. Nearby is the **Mill & Rural Life Museum** (www.bishopslydeardmill.co.uk) in Mill Lane, which dates from the eighteenth century and is a Grade II listed building equipped with an overshot waterwheel that was renovated and opened by the town's mayor in 2003. The wheel weighs more than two tons and is driven by water from **Back Stream**, which flows down from the Brendon Hills. The museum's focus is on traditional trades and crafts, including wheelwright, cooper, saddler and blacksmith, as well as a Victorian kitchen.

Continuing in the literary vein, and on the other side of the A358, is **Ash Priors**, the former home of science fiction writer Arthur C. Clarke, who lived at Ballifants Farm, on the village outskirts. Other notable residents were Henry and Elizabeth Wolcott, emigrants to New England and great-grandparents of Oliver Wolcott, one of the signatories of the US Declaration of Independence.

A series of lanes is probably the quickest way to reach the next point of interest, the town of **Milverton**, but we can also take a longer route by heading from Ash Priors back onto the A358, heading towards Taunton; take the B3227 before reaching the town, and follow this road until you see the relevant signs. If you take this second way, just after turning onto the smaller road, you will go through the village of **Norton Fitzwarren** with its hillfort. The site was first occupied in the Neolithic era era, but the surviving banks are part of the Bronze and later Iron Age fortifications. The edges of the fort are wooded and form a crown on top of the hill in which can be found oak, ash and sycamore trees. Much of the flora is dominated by ivy, but some ancient woodland plants such as bluebell and wood anemone can be found. It is said a red dragon lived on the hill at the time of the Roman Conquest and its likeness can be seen carved in stone in the parish church. Also located in the village lies the recently built **Somerset Archives and Local Studies Centre** (www.swheritage.org.uk) better known by its original name as the Somerset Record Office, which holds the archives for the entire county along with many archaeological collections in a superb purpose-built series of buildings at the village's Brunel Way. The records include oral historical recordings, estate and manorial records, parish registers and the archives of Somerset Light Infantry and Avon & Somerset Constabulary.

History of the County Archives

Somerset can claim a longer continuously known history of official record keeping than any other county in England. A meeting of Quarter Sessions held at Wells in 1617 decided that a room should be provided 'for the safe keeping of the records of the Sessions'. By 1619 Somerset possessed not only its own record room, but also a room adjoining for the use of searchers. The record room stood next to the Chain Gate on the north side of Wells Cathedral and remained in use for the next 200 years.

A short-lived successor was found in premises at Wilton Gaol, Taunton, in 1817, before the records were consigned to Shire Hall, which opened in 1858. The Somerset County Council was formed in 1889 and its Clerk became custodian of the records. A Records Committee of the County Council was appointed in 1901, and in 1907, the first Local Record Officer, a part-time post, was chosen.

Once the accommodation at Shire Hall was refitted, it was approved by the Master of the Rolls as a repository for manorial documents in 1931. It was then possible for the fledgling Record Office to preserve not only the county's official records, but also the records of private individuals, landed families, and corporate bodies.

After the Second World War, the Record Office struggled with the large increase in records being deposited, notably, major estate collections. The need for a purpose-built repository was recognised by the County Council, and the new Somerset Record Office was opened in 1958. The design of the building was carefully matched to the varied needs of archive preservation, archive storage, and the use of archives in the public search-room.

In the twenty-first century, there has been, once again, the need to increase the quantity and quality of storage space for Somerset's archives. Since December 2003, the Record Office has also been part of Somerset County Council's Heritage Group, along with Museums, Historic Environment and the Victoria County History.

In 2010, the Record Office moved to new, purpose-built premises at the Somerset Heritage Centre, Brunel Way, Norton Fitzwarren, Taunton, TA2 6SF. This brought together the Archives, Local Studies, Museums, Historic Environment and Victoria County History departments. [Extracted from Somerset Heritage Centre website]

It is now time to move on to **Milverton** (www.milverton-somerset.uk) itself. Neolithic flint arrowheads and Bronze Age axe heads have been discovered in its locale, while the **Old House** – now a Grade II listed building and possibly dating from the late fourteenth century – was once the home of Thomas Cranmer, Archbishop of Canterbury at the time of Henry VIII. A mural depicting the monarch which has been dated to around 1541 was uncovered on the wall in the house in 2011 and there is speculation that the image contains a secret message. Perhaps Milverton's best claim to historical fame, however, is that it was the birthplace of scientist Thomas Young. Born in the village in 1773, Young went on to make notable contributions in many different scientific fields, securing a reputation as a polymath (a person whose expertise spans a significant number of subject areas). His work on the decipherment of Egyptian hieroglyphics and specifically the Rosetta Stone laid the foundation for Jean-Francois Champollion's ultimate breakthrough.

Whether coming from Wiveliscombe or Milverton, the next historical point of interest to head towards is **Wellington** (www.wellingtonsomerset. com). It has been said that this small market town, six miles southwest of Taunton, has an 'appealing sleepy, old-fashioned air, almost detached from modern life'. True or not, its museum is certainly worth the stop and the place itself can be used as base for nearby attractions, of which there are several. Exhibits in the **Wellington Museum**, (www.wellingtonmuseum. org.uk) at 28 Fore Street, feature famous firms and individuals, past and present, based in the town. There are displays about the Duke of Wellington – along with the nearby monument to him – the English Civil War, the Howards, Foxes, and John Wesley, to name just a few. The museum is run by a knowledgeable team of volunteers, who also organise local walks, and there is a comprehensive range of books and leaflets on the town.

The **Wellington Monument** (www.nationaltrust.org.uk/wellington-monument) is a triangular obelisk located on a point of the Blackdown Hills about two miles south of the town. It is a Grade II listed building designed to commemorate the Duke of Wellington's victory at the Battle of Waterloo. Following his earlier victory at the Battle of Talavera, Arthur Wellesley was ennobled, but as he was abroad at the time, his brother chose the name of the Somerset town, because of its similarity to the family name, although neither Wellesley had ever visited it. Parliament awarded Arthur £100,000, and with this he bought two manors in the town, including the land upon which the monument stands. The monument was proposed in 1815 by William Sanford of Nynehead Court, who started a public subscription to pay for it. Within months £1,450 had been raised and a design competition was held. The winning entry envisaged a 95ft pillar with three cottages at its base to house old soldiers as caretakers. Designed by Thomas Lee, the foundation stone was laid by Lord Somerville in 1817. By 1818 the column was 47ft high, but funds were exhausted, so a revised, and cheaper design was decided upon. Another appeal raised further funds and the column was raised 74ft. It was damaged in 1846, when struck by lightning, and construction did not restart until after the duke's death; it was finally completed by Henry Goodridge in 1854.

The design was inspired by an Egyptian obelisk, but in the shape of the type of bayonet used by Wellington's armies. The upper section was restored in 1890 when the pinnacle was raised by 5ft. The original plans were for twenty-four cannons, captured from the French at Waterloo, to be installed around the base, with a cast iron statue of the duke on the top and more statues on the plinth, but these were never built. In 1818, one brass and fifteen iron cannons were transported from the Royal Arsenal at Woolwich to Exeter Quay, but never made it to the monument. After years of storage at Exeter, ten of them were sunk into the ground as bollards, and the brass gun sold off in 1837 for £64, to cover the storage costs incurred by the local corporation. In 1890, when four guns were requested for the monument as part of a restoration project, they were found to be naval cannons cast in Scotland dating from 1789 and never used at the Battle of Waterloo. Four cannons were eventually installed in 1910, but these were removed during the Second World War for scrap metal in a propaganda exercise to help the war effort and when the metal they were made of proved to be useless for military purposes they were buried at Watchet. The one remaining cannon at Exeter was brought to the monument in the late 1970s and installed in 1984.

The column is built of local stone and is 80ft wide at the base and 175ft in height. The base has an Egyptian winged panel above the studded iron door and is surmounted by a coved dentil cornice. A counterweight hangs inside the top of the monument to help balance it in windy weather,

The Wellington Monument. © Chris Andrews (cc-by-sa/2.0)

while an internal staircase ascends to a viewing platform, which has three circular windows, one on each face.

The monument was acquired by the National Trust in the 1930s and is floodlit on special occasions. The Rotary Club donated the cannon currently standing at the monument's base. It was closed to the public in 2007 amid safety concerns, surveys having shown that extensive renovation work would be needed in order to reopen the internal staircase. In June 2009, plans were announced to re-clad the monument at a cost of £4 million. A painted fence was replaced by an open wire fence in 2010, aiding visibility, but still denying public access to the base. Survey work that same year showed the extent of cracks in the stonework and in 2013 it was announced that further funding would be needed for the restoration project; this was refused in October 2017 and at the time of writing, no further action is planned.

One of the attractions close to Wellington is the fifteenth-century medieval house **Cothay Manor** (www.cothaymanor.co.uk) and gardens, built around 1480 and a Grade I listed building. Considered by many to be the most perfect of all the small, classic medieval dwellings within England, it rated four stars in Simon Jenkins' *England's Thousand Best Houses*. Its gate piers and wall to the north entrance are themselves listed Grade II. The rent for the land surrounding the manor in the medieval era was a pair of silver spurs and a rose. To celebrate the end of the Wars of the Roses, in the Tudor iconography of the time, a red rose (for Lancashire), and a white rose (for Yorkshire) were planted on the terrace by Richard Bluett, who was the lord of the manor at the time.

The gardens were designed and laid out by Colonel Reginald Cooper DSO in the 1920s, who was an old friend of Sissinghurst Castle garden owner Sir Harold Nicolson, a fellow pupil at Wellington College, Berkshire and the pair served together within the Diplomatic Corps. They in turn were friends of another brilliant garden innovator, Major Lawrence Johnston of Hidcote Manor and the architect Edwin Lutyens. These gardeners exchanged ideas and in Nicholson's diaries there is an entry: 'Reggie came to stay and advised me on the length of the bowling green'. Sissinghurst itself was laid out in 1932, with one garden writer describing Cothay as the 'Sissinghurst of the West Country'.

Cider: The Champagne of the West Country

The origins of cider making in the West Country are not fully known. Orchards certainly existed here in Roman times or before and it seems strange that they would not have hit upon such a simple process, but the fact remains that the first written reference we have of cider in Britain comes from around 1160 and relates to an orchard in Canterbury. Whatever its origins in the Somerset area it has certainly been made here for hundreds of years and is still very popular. The drink is produced from apples turned into a pulp which has the consistency of apple sauce and is known as 'pomace'. The pomace from different apple varieties is selected according to taste, is then mixed together and formed into a large block known as a 'cheese'. The cheese is then pressed until all the juice has been squeezed out and the resulting liquid is left to ferment. Cider made by the traditional method has no extra yeast added to it and the fermentation process starts within one to two days and continues for several weeks after which it matures for five to six months. Traditional cider is properly served completely flat and maybe cloudy with an alcoholic content around 6 per cent.

Some Proper Somerset Cider Producers

Roger Wilkins, Lands' End Farm, Mudgley, Wedmore, BS28 4TU. 01934 712 385 – The king of Somerset cider makers and something of a tourist attraction in his own right, Roger pours his pure and natural cider straight from the wood, dry or sweet, if you want medium, he will mix the two together for you. As Roger says, 'The farm is open seven days a week from 10.00 until 8.00, 'cept Sundays when we close at 1.00 pm, so I can have a quiet Sunday lunch.' – www.wilkinscider.com

Rich's Cider, Mill House, Watchfield, Highbridge, TA9 4RD. 01278 783 651 – Still making traditional cider in a proper way after over fifty years and still family run but now diversifying into more commercial types with the addition of a top-rated restaurant supplying locally produced food. Their traditional Farmhouse comes in dry, medium and sweet – www.richscider.co.uk

Hecks Farmhouse Cider, 9-11 Middle Leigh, Street, BA16 0LB. 01458 442 367 – The Hecks family have been making traditional farmhouse cider in Somerset for six generations since 1841, blending juice from apples all grown locally in the farm's orchards which is then fermented in wooden barrels and sold draught from the wood. In 1896, they started to sell their cider from the farm shop in Street and still do so today, having diversified into a number of single varieties as well as the traditional farmhouse – www.heckscider.com

Perry's Real Somerset Cider, Dowlish Wake, Ilminster, TA19 ONY. 01460 52681 – The Perry family have been making award winning craft ciders since 1920 when William Churchill acquired the family farm and started making cider as a sideline to his blacksmith's business. The company was later taken over by Henry and Bert Perry, his nephews who pushed the company forward and continued to experiment with craft ciders. The family still ferment their ciders in the same way and continue to use the two hydraulic presses installed in the 50s. These presses have squeezed over 7 million pints of cider each. Traditional farmhouse cider is available along with the fizzy stuff in bottles – www. perryscider.co.uk

Worley's Cider, 55, Dean, Shepton Mallet, BA4 4SA. 01749 880016 – Worley's describe themselves as a 'hobby that got out of control' a few years ago, and now they make 30,000 litres a year. Many bottled varieties as well as a farmhouse – www.worleyscider.co.uk

Burrow Hill Cider Company, Pass Vale Farm, Burrow Hill, Martock, TA12 6BU. 01460 240 782 – Julian Temperley, maker of the famed Cider Brandy at Burrow Hill where cider has been made for over 200 years. Many bottled varieties as well as a traditional farmhouse cider – www.somersetciderbrandy.com

It is now time to head towards Taunton itself, but not before stopping on the way to learn more about the drink most associated with this county. Somerset is known the world over for the making of cider – the fermented juice of apples – and one of the well-known, present-day exponents is Sheppy's, which has been located at Bradford-on-Tone (around 3.5 miles southwest of Taunton) since the family moved there in 1917. **Sheppy's Cider Farm** (www.sheppyscider.com) is well worth a visit to see how cider is made in the twenty-first century – a far cry from its traditional craft origins, which are considered in a later chapter, but the farm shop, tea room, orchards and museum are worth a visit.

Close by is **Bradford Bridge** (www.ancientmonuments.uk/104441-bradford-bridge-bradford-on-tone) which carries a road over the River Tone and was built between the thirteenth and fifteenth centuries. By 1667 it had been adopted as a 'County Bridge' and a marker stone has been installed to show which side of the bridge was the responsibility of which local Justice of the Peace. The two-arch stone bridge was restored in 1698 and again in the late nineteenth century. In 2000, however, a lorry went through the parapet of the bridge, which resulted in the collapse of a whole section. It is now a scheduled ancient monument and listed building.

We now arrive at **Taunton** (www.visitsomerset.co.uk/taunton) and despite all the fascinating history that surrounds it in the outlying areas, this major regional town has also witnessed its fair share of important historical events since being founded as a military camp in the eighth century by the Saxon King Ine. These include hostilities during the War of the Roses, three Civil War sieges, doomed challenges to the English crown and the bloody retribution that followed these failed attempts to usurp the reigning monarch. One of these attempts occurred towards the end of the fifteenth century. History knows **Perkin Warbeck** as a failed pretender and imposter to the throne of England, although even today mystery still surrounds his real identity. Claiming to be Richard of Shrewsbury (Duke of York and one of the 'Princes in the Tower') he led an uprising to oust Henry VII and take his place. Landing at Whitesand Bay, near Land's End, in September 1497, the 120 men Warbeck brought with him soon swelled to 6,000 – mainly Cornishmen – in what became known as the Second Cornish Uprising. By the end of the month his 'army' reached Taunton, but on hearing the king's

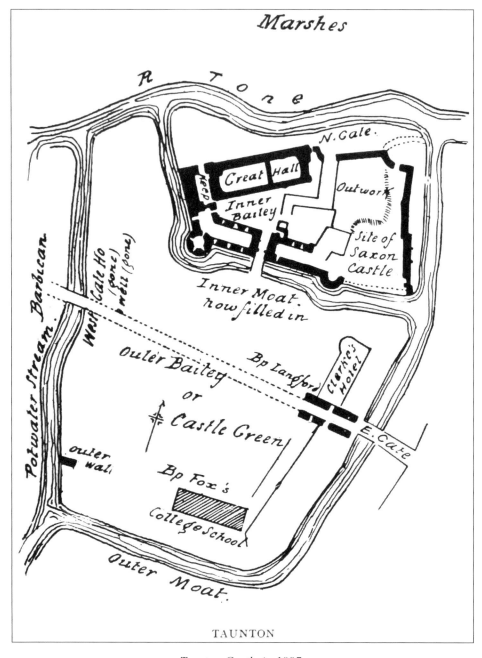

Taunton Castle in 1897.

forces were on their way to confront it, Warbeck deserted his men. Henry VII arrived in the town on 4 October to accept the rebel army's surrender and oversaw the execution of its remaining ringleaders. As for Perkin 'King Richard' Warbeck, he was imprisoned at Taunton, having been captured in Hampshire, and after his trial there, he was paraded through the streets of London on horseback before being executed by hanging at Tyburn.

One of the town's most significant attractions is **Taunton Castle**, which stands on Taunton Green. Although thought to be Anglo-Saxon in origin, much of its current structure dates from the medieval period. The building was much repaired during the Civil War, when Taunton was captured by the Parliamentary forces and became their only base in the southwest. A few years later the castle was the scene of Judge Jeffries and his 'Bloody Assizes', which took place after the defeat of the Monmouth Rebellion. By the late eighteenth century parts of the castle had fallen into disrepair and were restored in the Georgian style. **Castle Bow** is the last remaining gate to the castle. This was the castle's east gate and was originally approached over a drawbridge. A replica portcullis has been installed in the original medieval grooves.

Taunton Castle. © Philip Halling (cc-by-sa/2.0)

The **Museum of Somerset**, housed within the Great Hall of Taunton Castle, (www.swheritage.org.uk/museum-of-somerset/explore/taunton-castle) dates from around the twelfth century. Exhibits include objects collected by the Somerset Archaeological and Natural History Society, who purchased the building 1874. In 1900, the Great Hall was repaired and refitted for the museum's use, and eight years later the **Adam Library** was created to house the society's growing collection of books. The museum's artefacts include a collection of toys and dolls, sculpture, natural history, fossils, fine silver, ancient pottery, a shrunken head from South America, Judge Jeffreys's medical bill, the Low Ham Roman Mosaic, the Bronze Age South Cadbury shield, and a range of other objects and items relating to the history and archaeology of the county. The building also houses the **Somerset Military Museum**, (www.swheritage.org.uk/museum-of-somerset/explore/somerset-military-museum) where visitors can follow the fortunes of the Somerset Light Infantry as they carried out their campaigns across the world.

One of the museum's prize exhibits, however, is the **Frome Hoard**, a collection of 52,503 Roman coins discovered at Witham Friary in April 2010, near Frome, by metal detectorist Dave Crisp. The coins were contained in a ceramic pot 18in in diameter, and date from AD 253 to 305. Most of the coins are made from debased silver or bronze and the hoard is one of the largest discovered in Britain. The pot's contents included the largest group of coins yet discovered that were issued during the reign of Carausius, who ruled Britain independently from AD 286 to 293 and was the first Roman emperor to strike coins in Britain.

Moving on from the museum, we come to the **Tudor House**, at 15 Fore Street, which is reputed to be the oldest house in the town. The timber framed three-storey house was built in 1578, with jettied first and second floors. At one time it was the property of Sir William Portman, who escorted the ill-fated Duke of Monmouth to London for his trial and execution, following his failed rebellion. The interior has been greatly altered over the years, but the great hall with its trussed roof survives. After many years as a grocer's and an antique shop, the building lay empty for a long time before being refurbished at a reputed cost of £200,000 and leased to Caffè Nero in 2003.

Also located in Fore Street is the **Market House,** a red-brick Georgian building standing at the southern end of North Street, facing the **Burma Memorial**. The Market House was built in 1772 by architect Coplestone Warre Bampfylde, who is probably best known for the elegant gardens at Hestercombe. The Market House was designed for various uses, with separate areas for administration of justice and amusement; the ground floor served as the Guildhall, where magistrates heard weekly court cases, while the first floor was a galleried assembly room for musical functions. In 1929, the market moved, and the ground-floor arcades were removed so new wings could be added, which included the one which houses the **Tourist Information Centre** (www.visitsomerset.co.uk/visitor-information/taunton-visitor-centre). The Burma Memorial was moved to its present location in 1996 and is nominally the centre of historical Taunton; a striking memorial that stands on a traffic island at the junction of North Street, Hammet Street and Fore Street. The monument commemorates the men of Prince Albert's Somersetshire Light Infantry who fell in the Third Burma War of 1885–87. It is in the style of a tall Celtic cross standing on a stepped plinth. Near the base are carved the battle honours of Egypt, Burma, Azim Curh, and Jellalabad. During the Burmese conflict 144 men of the Somerset Light Infantry's 2nd Battalion lost their lives.

Somerset is one of England's great cricketing counties and another of Taunton's museums, **The Somerset Cricket Museum**, (www.somersetcountycc.co.uk) at 7, Priory Avenue, chronicles this legendary team's various achievements. The location of the museum within the town is not surprising, as Taunton is home to the Somerset County Cricket Club, as well as England's Women's Cricket Association. The exhibits and displays in the museum cover the club's history, including such famous former players as Ian Botham, Viv Richards and Marcus Trescothick. The building in which the museum is housed is the only remaining part of the Augustinian Priory that was founded here in about 1115, and it is possible its early use was as a guesthouse or quarters for a priory official. The local stone rubble has been repaired with red brick capped by a tie-beam roof covered with tiles. The door and window openings are made of Bishops Lydeard stone. The exact date of the building is disputed, but it is argued to be from the late fifteenth or early sixteenth century, which replaced an

The Burma Memorial © Stephen McKay (cc-by-sa/2.0)

earlier thirteenth or fourteenth-century building. It is also thought to have been used as a chapel by French prisoners during the French Revolutionary Wars. The **Old Priory Barn**, as it is known, was purchased by the Somerset CCC Supporters Club when it became available in 1979, as the club itself did not have the funds at the time and after a ten-year restoration it was opened to the public in April 1989.

St Mary Magdalene Church, in Church Square, has the highest tower in Somerset at 163ft, and the views from the top are superb. There has been a church here since the twelfth century. Of note is the painted monument to Robert Gray a town alderman who established the alms-houses on East Street and died in 1635.

It is now time to leave Taunton, and for lovers of historical gardens, the A38 between Taunton and Bridgwater gives a further treat in this section. **Hestercombe Gardens** (www.hestercombe.com) at **Cheddon Fitzpaine** is a mix of three historic gardens and is the happy result of a collaboration between Sir Edwin Lutyens and Gertrude Jekyll, who created a formal Edwardian garden within the larger 40-acre Georgian one originally designed by Copelstone Warre Bampfylde, a friend of Henry Hoare of Stourhead. The overall site includes woodland walks, a classical temple, waterfalls and breathtaking views across the Vale of Taunton.

The Hestercombe estate dates to at least the eleventh century, when it was owned by Glastonbury Abbey, while the current manor house dates to the sixteenth century and was built for the Warre family. The house was extended in the eighteenth century, and then comprehensively rebuilt in 1875, by Edward Portman, 1st Viscount Portman. The Victorian facade hides the earlier historic core of the building. As mentioned above, the grounds surrounding the house were laid out in the late eighteenth century as a fashionable landscape garden in typical Georgian style with neo-classical follies, water features, and a great cascade. It is said that Jekyll was one of the first gardeners to incorporate colour theory to garden design and drew on the works of impressionist painters as well as using texture as an essential ingredient in the laying out of a garden. Her collaboration with Lutyens on this project has resulted in Hestercombe becoming a triumph that has influenced a generation of gardeners.

Other points of interest in the area include **Castle Neroche** a Norman-built motte-and-bailey type castle on the site of an earlier hill fort in the parish of Curland, near Staple Fitzpaine. The hill rises to 850ft on the northern escarpment of the Blackdown Hills. The area is part of a 35-square mile site covered by a landscape partnership, known as the Neroche Scheme, which is establishing trails and a public forest. The origin of the term 'Neroche' is believed to be a contraction of an Old English word for a type of hunting-dog used in Britain in the Middle Ages, meaning that the camp was a place where hunting dogs were kept.

Cothelstone Manor (www.cothelstonemanor.co.uk) six miles to the north of Taunton, at the foot of the Quantock Hills, is not open to the general public, but private tours can be arranged with its owners under the 'Invitation to View' scheme. This is well worth doing as it is a beautiful late Elizabethan Manor parts of which may date back to Saxon times. It did suffer badly during the English Civil War though, when its then owner Sir John Stawell backed the wrong side. Cromwell ordered the manor to be destroyed by cannon fire and it was greatly reduced in size and has never fully recovered. A little later, Judge Jeffries hanged several Monmouth rebels found guilty at his Bloody Assizes from the manor gateway, as an example to any who might seek to oppose the king.

The nearby **St Agnes's Well** is a Grade II well-house dating from the medieval period and restored in the nineteenth century. It sits nestled in a field to the north-east of the manor house and by the side of the road from Bishop's Lydeard to Bagborough. and is constructed of coursed red sandstone masonry with a corbelled roof. Its water is accessed via an arched doorway, behind which is a large volume of clear shallow water piped off for farm use. It has a varied folklore; as well as being a healing and wishing well of considerable power, it is also supposedly an aid to fertility. In addition, virgins use divinations to 'discover' their future husbands on the eve of St Agnes's feast day. However, many local people do not take advantage of these benefits because it is also the place where mischievous pixies live as it lies close to the 'Pixie Stream'. The site is in the process of further restoration.

The next stop is Coates English Willow **Willows & Wetlands Visitor's Centre** (www.englishwillowbaskets.co.uk) at Meare Green Court,

Stoke St Gregory, is located on a working farm. The centre offers tours of more than 80 acres of withies and willow yards as well as explaining the history of willow on the Somerset Levels. The latter features exhibits relating to willow growing, processing and basket-making, a video room describing the industry and a basket museum with displays of traditional and unusual willow artefacts. **The Levels and Moors Exhibition** describes the history of the surrounding local countryside and its links with this traditional industry, while an environmental interpretation display highlights the importance of water in shaping the Levels. The centre is owned and run by the Coate family, who have been growing willow on the Somerset Levels since 1819 and making baskets since 1904. During the Victorian era wicker furniture became popular; it was believed to be more sanitary as it collected less dust than upholstery. Large numbers of people were employed in the industry, many as 'outworkers', processing the willow in their own homes.

Ancient earthwork **Balt Moor Wall** (www.historicengland.org.uk/listing) at Lyng, also on the Somerset Levels, lies to the northwest of the River Tone. The site contains the remains of a section of medieval causeway that now forms a raised embankment between 20 and 33ft wide and almost 7ft high. The structure, which English Heritage refers to as 'a rare example of medieval engineering', appears to have been built to protect the salt moor from the flooding of the River Tone in the Athelney-Lyng gap. The wall is first mentioned in a charter signed by King Stephen between 1135 and 1154, when monks from Athelney Abbey were reclaiming some of the land. The original construction may date from the ninth century, but it is not clear whether this was intended to control the course of the River Tone, or as a causeway between the fortified sites at Lyng and Isle of Athelney. The Somerset Drainage Commission ordered the causeway to be encased in masonry in 1880. In 1996 the wall was tested for stability, during which time medieval pottery was unearthed. Geophysical surveys were carried out in the late 1980s and early 1990s, with exploratory trenches being dug in 1996.

Athelney itself, located between the villages of Burrowbridge and East Lyng, is best known for once being the fortress hiding place of King Alfred the Great. After the Danes had attacked his royal stronghold

The Balt Moor Wall. © *Roger Cornfoot (cc-by-sa/2.0)*

in Chippenham in early 878, Alfred fled into Somerset and it was somewhere on the Somerset Levels that the legend of the 'burnt cakes' occurred. Given shelter by a peasant woman, who was unaware of his identity, she left him to watch some wheaten cakes cooking on the fire. Naturally preoccupied with the affairs of his kingdom, he accidentally let the cakes burn and was subsequently admonished by the woman on her return. Not long after this, Alfred the Great established a fortress at Athelney and this became the headquarters for the resistance movement against the Danish Army. This culminated in the Battle of Edington, in neighbouring Wiltshire, when Alfred's Anglo-Saxon army defeated the Great Heathen Army in May 878. At Atheleny, there is a monument to King Alfred.

The Gertrude Jekyll connection extends to another location within the area, this time it is **Barrington Court** (www.nationaltrust.org.uk/ barrington-court), a Tudor manor house begun in about 1538 and completed in the late 1550s, with a vernacular seventeenth-century stable court of 1675. It is also notable for being the first house acquired by the National Trust, in 1907, although it was later leased to Colonel Lyle of Tate & Lyle in the 1920s. The connection with Jekyll comes from its gardens in the Arts and Crafts style, for which the renowned garden designer provided planting plans.

A group of nine Bronze Age barrows, known as **Robin Hood's Butts** (www.stone-circles.org.uk/stone/robinhoodsbutts) stand near Otterford on the Blackdown Hills. They are all scheduled as ancient monuments. Two of the bowl barrows north-west of Brown Down Cottage are between 92ft and 289ft in diameter. The two 1,250ft west and 2,247ft north-west of Beech Croft are slightly larger, with one being 138ft and the other measures 144ft in diameter. The others are round barrows and are located 330ft south of School Farm. Four are bowl shaped and the other a bell barrow. They should all be visible from a public right of way, although there is no right of way to the barrows themselves.

Robin Hood's Butts © Roger Cornfoot (cc-by-sa/2.0)

Lying north of Pitminster is **Poundisford Park,** an English country house that typifies progressive house-building on the part of the West Country gentry in the mid-sixteenth century. The main house is Grade 1 listed and was built in around 1550. The three-storey house was extended with a dining room added to the northeast of the original house in 1692. In 1717, a stable, coach house and barn were added, with the service wing to the south-east of the main block being added between 1717 and 1823. The house is approximately H-shaped with entrances placed to the north and south and was influenced by another Somerset mansion, Barrington Court. In addition to several buildings, the grounds contain formal gardens laid out in the seventeenth century and set within a medieval deer park. In 1534 this park was divided into two, with the northern section including the original lodge, leased to Roger Hill, whose son rebuilt it. The southern area, without a house, was leased to a William Soper who built the present Poundisford Park. The great hall of the house rises in the traditional way through two storeys and occupies the central bar of the H-plan. Its entrance porch rises through the facade to a gable that is matched on the opposite side with an oriel window similarly rising through both floors to a matching gable. A central gable in the recessed central bay reinforces the symmetry of the entrance front. The two halves were 'reunited' in 1869, when the park was sold to the Helyer family – who already owned the lodge – but only remained intact for sixty years, before the estate was sold off in 1928 for £10,000. **Poundisford Lodge,** which predates the Park, is around 2,000ft north of the main house. This two-storey building is U-shaped, with the hall range extending from north to south and lateral wings extending to the north-west and south-west. The lodge contains two fine-looking late-sixteenth-century plasterwork barrel-vaulted bedrooms and extensive decorative wainscoting.

Lying in the parish of Hatch Beauchamp is **Hatch Court**, a stunning mansion built in the Palladian style by a successful wool merchant John Collins in around 1755. The main house has two storeys and is built of Bath stone with four square corner towers of three storeys. The gardens have a walled vegetable section and once contained a pleasure garden which included a grotto with a fireplace and pool.

We have now come to the end of this section and so it is time to head northward to the Sedgemoor district, which has among its highlights the site of the last battle fought on English soil.

Food and Drink

Plough Inn, 75 Station Road, Taunton, TA1 1PB. 01823 324404 – Four locally brewed real ales are served along with seven Somerset ciders. Wooden-floored and stone-walled, the split-level bar areas are furnished with sofas and armchairs and a selection of board games are available. Ideally situated close to the railway station and cricket ground, it's a favourite haunt of cricket fans. Pub food consists of a varied selection of pies and a choice of granary baguettes. Somerset CAMRA cider pub of the year 2013 – www.theploughtaunton.co.uk

Winchester Arms, Castle Green, TA1 4AD. 01823 272488 – Town-centre pub next door to bus station, giving easy access from various locations in and around Taunton. Family friendly with restaurant area. TV sports and live music – www.winchesterarmstauntonpub.co.uk

Bird in Hand, 34 Mount Street, Bishops Lydeard, TA4 3LH. 01823 432090 – A family run country pub in the heart of the village at the foot of the Quantock hills and just a 10-minute walk from the West Somerset Heritage Railway. Dogs and muddy boots are welcome at this family friendly pub. Five local and south-west brewery ales on hand pumps. Home-cooked locally sourced food. The slate floor bar has a cosy log-burner fire. There is a skittle alley which is available for functions, and a large beer garden at the rear of the pub provides an ideal setting in the summer.

Lethbridge Arms, Gore Square, Bishops Lydeard. 01823 433467 – Sixteenth century coaching inn in an attractive village at the foot of the Quantock hills. Popular with locals and near the West Somerset Railway, the pub provides good, locally sourced food and has accommodation. Frequently used by railway enthusiasts, there are numerous photographs and paintings of maps and railway scenes – www.thelethbridgearmspub.co.uk

The Dolphin, 37 Waterloo Road Wellington, TA21 8JQ. 01823 665889 – Traditional town centre pub serving up to four local ales on weekends. Home-cooked food served daily, plus pizzas to eat in or take away. These include vegan and gluten-free varieties. Live music twice a month, normally on Thursdays or Saturdays, and monthly themed food or charity nights. The colourful pub frontage is an unusual mural featuring handpumps depicting local breweries and wine bottles – www.thedolphinwellington.co.uk

White Horse Inn, Regent Street, Bradford-on-Tone, TA4 1HF. 01823 461239 – This friendly village pub is very much a community affair, housing the local shop run by villagers in outbuildings. The bar and restaurant are both heated by real fires in winter. The beautiful large garden hosts barbecues in summer. Excellent food is locally sourced and home cooked, and themed food nights are held. Regular events include music jam sessions, quiz nights and table-top sales. The skittle alley doubles as a function room – www.whitehorseinn.pub

CHAPTER 3

Sedgemoor District

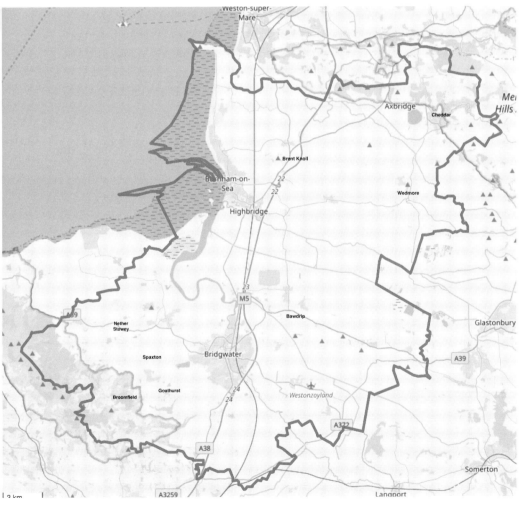

Map of Sedgemoor District.

The name **Sedgemoor** will be forever linked with the ill-fated rebellion of the Duke of Monmouth and his defeat there in 1685, but this low-lying area that runs across the coastal plain of central Somerset, from the Quantock hills to the Mendips, was also the place in which King Alfred took refuge in the ninth century and reorganised his forces, before successfully defending his kingdom against the Danish Vikings at the battle of Edington.

To the north of Taunton, and the first major location within this section is the town of **Bridgwater** (www.bridgwatertown.com). Both towns have had many links over the centuries; one of which was by water in the form of the **Bridgwater and Taunton Canal** (www.canalrivertrust.org.uk) which opened in 1827, linking the River Tone to the River Parrett. There were several abortive schemes to link the Bristol and English Channels by waterway in the late eighteenth and early nineteenth centuries and these schemes followed the approximate route eventually taken by the Bridgwater and Taunton Canal, which was built as part of a plan to link Bristol to Taunton. The early years of operation were marred by several legal disputes, which were only resolved when the Bridgwater and Taunton Canal Company and Conservators, who managed the River Tone Navigation, agreed the Canal Company should take over the running of the Tone Navigation. The canal originally terminated at a basin at Huntworth, to the east of Bridgwater, but was later extended to a floating harbour at Bridgwater Docks on its western edge. Financially this was a disaster, as the extension was funded by a mortgage, and the arrival of the railways soon afterwards ensured the canal's demise. It was rescued from bankruptcy by the Bristol and Exeter Railway in 1866 and despite commercial traffic ceasing in 1907, the infrastructure was maintained in good order, and the canal was used for the transport of potable water from 1962. The Countryside Act 1968 provided a framework for Somerset County Council to start the restoration of the canal as a leisure facility, which was completed in 1994. Bridgwater lies at the northern end of the Bridgwater and Taunton Canal. Although it is a large historic market town and has been a major inland port and trading centre since the industrial revolution, its neighbour, Taunton is the bigger of the two. As well as being historically linked for centuries by the canal, the pair were later connected by the railway and then most recently, the M5 motorway. Regarding the railway, **Bridgwater Railway Station** lies on the Bristol to

Taunton line and covers more than 150 miles from London Paddington via Bristol's Temple Meads. Built to the designs of Isambard Kingdom Brunel, the station is today a Grade II listed building. The railway first opened in Bridgwater on 14 June 1841, when the Bristol & Exeter Railway (although its parent company was the GWR) opened its line and was the terminus for a year, before the line was extended down to Taunton. During its time as a terminus, Bridgwater became a focus for horse-drawn coaches which met the trains and carried their passengers on to their final destinations.

The coke ovens, which provided fuel for the locomotives, and the workshops which built and maintained the carriages and wagons, lay to the west of the line between Bridgwater station and the river. A fire in 1947 caused their closure although by this time they were only used for repairing the canvas covers for the wagons. Another local industry linked to the railway was **John Browne's Brick and Tile Works**, owned by a director of the railway which supplied materials to the Great Western and associated companies. George Hennet's iron works was another, making track, signals and wagons for several different companies including atmospheric railway pipes for South Devon Railway Company. The station was renovated on several occasions; in 1882, new roofs and a footbridge were provided, and in 1893 an engine shed was added outside the carriage works. Following the nationalisation of the railways in 1948 stations in many towns were renamed to avoid confusion, and this one became Bridgwater Central in 1949 to distinguish it from Bridgwater North, the former Somerset and Dorset Joint Railway terminus.

In July 1960 the engine shed closed and shunting locomotives were brought up from Taunton as and when they were needed. The decline continued with goods traffic being withdrawn from November 1965; when the docks branch and Dunball Wharf closed in 1967, the goods yard was 'rationalised' and most of the sidings that had served the former carriage works at the south end of the station were taken out of use by 1969. Despite all the gloom, the station buildings have managed to survive in reasonable repair and the modernised booking office retains a rare early ticket counter. The main entrance lies on the town side of the station and the platform served by trains towards Bristol and access to the platform for trains towards Taunton is by a footbridge.

Elsewhere within the town is **Bridgwater Museum**, otherwise known as the **Blake Museum** (www.bridgwatermuseum.org.uk) which is situated at 5 Blake Street, down a quiet back street of the town and a short distance from the centre. The Grade II listed building which was built in the late fifteenth or early sixteenth century is believed to be the birthplace of the town's most famous citizen, Robert Blake, General at Sea (1598–1657). The museum was founded in 1926 by the local council but is now run, very successfully, by the town council and a team of volunteers. Among the museum's collections, are artefacts from Blake's life, including his sea chest. The building also doubles as the local museum for the archaeology and history of Bridgwater and surrounding areas. which includes much on the Battle of Sedgemoor. Adjoining the museum is **Blake Gardens** which opened in 1902 and is a good example of a municipal garden of that period.

Also within the town is **King Square,** which was developed with large Georgian houses in the late eighteenth century on the site of Bridgwater Castle and built by John Harvey. The remains of the castle and land was sold to James Brydges, 1st Duke of Chandos, who developed an industrial centre in the town and demolished the last of the buildings. Much of the site was built on in the 1720s to create the Georgian Castle Street. In 1734, Chandos sold the whole of the redevelopment area to Thomas Watts, who subsequently sold it on after only a year to John Anderton, whose descendants continued to clear old buildings and construct new ones.

Standing in King Square is the impressive bronze **Bridgwater War Memorial** (www.roll-of-honour.com/Somerset/Bridgwater, which was designed by John Angel in the mid-1920s. The figure is allegorical, representing civilisation as a seated woman, holding a globe in one hand and the book of knowledge on her lap.

Somerset Brick & Tile Museum (www.swheritage.org.uk/our-sites/brick-and-tile-museum**)** on East Quay illustrates the local industry of brick- and tile-making, one of the many labour-intensive coal-based industries that was at one time found in Somerset. At the heart of the museum is the only remaining pinnacle tile-kiln in Bridgwater, which used to be one of six at the former Barham Brothers' yard at East Quay and was last fired in 1965, the year that the works closed. In the 1840s this ancient trade employed over 1,300 people in the Bridgwater area. Demonstrated inside

Bridgwater War Memorial. © Neil Owen (cc-by-sa/2.0)

are the methods and processes involved in making the impressive variety of bricks, tiles, terracotta plaques and other wares that create the 'look' of Somerset towns like Bridgwater, Burnham and Glastonbury. The museum's kiln is a Scheduled Ancient Monument that was saved from dereliction in the 1990s, when it became part of the museum.

To the east of Bridgwater is a trio of historical landmarks. The first is **Burrow Mumps**, which is a hill and historic site overlooking Southlake Moor, near the village of Burrowbridge, and about eight miles from Bridgwater. It is a scheduled monument with a ruined church on top of the hill, built in 1793, that is Grade II listed. The area was donated to the National Trust, along with some surrounding land, in 1946 as a war memorial. The hill stands at a strategic location overlooking the point where the River Tone, and the old course of the River Cary, join the River Parrett. Although there is evidence of Roman visitation, the first known fortification of the site was the construction of a Norman motte. It has been called King Alfred's Fort but there is no proof he was here.

The Monmouth Rebellion

James Scott, the 1st Duke of Monmouth, was the eldest illegitimate son of Charles II and despite rumours Charles had married his mother, Lucy Walter, Charles always claimed that he had only ever had one wife, Catherine of Braganza. Charles died on 6 February 1685 and his elder brother James, a Catholic, became king. Monmouth was a Protestant and claimed the throne as rightfully his. He had been in self-imposed exile in the Dutch Republic, but feeling it was time to assert this right, he made plans to return to England.

On 11 June 1685, Monmouth landed at Lyme Regis, in Dorset, with a band of fewer than 100 supporters. His cause had always been popular in the West Country though, which was thought of as a strongly Protestant region, and it was among this population he planned to recruit his troops. Within the next few weeks he gathered together an ill-armed and ragged army of farm workers, peasants and nonconformists who planned to take control of the area before marching on London.

James, Duke of Monmouth.

Sadly, for Monmouth, King James II had already received information about the proposed attempt to overthrow him and in the days that followed the rebels engaged in several low-level skirmishes with local militias and elements of the regular army. On 15 June, Monmouth succeeded in taking Axminster, Devon, near the Somerset border, and gained more recruits bringing his force to around 6,000 men. On 20 June he had himself crowned in Taunton (Chapter 2) before moving north through Bridgwater (Chapter 3), Glastonbury and Shepton Mallet (Chapter 5) towards his goal of Bristol, then the country's second largest city.

Believing the city to be more heavily fortified than it was, and after a skirmish at Keynsham (Chapter 6), he moved east towards Bath, but unable to enter this city either, camped overnight at Norton St Phillip (Chapter 5). The result of the battle here was inconclusive, and Monmouth marched overnight to Frome, with the intention of camping there before heading on to the town of Warminster to gain more recruits. While in Frome (Chapter 5), he learnt a simultaneous rebellion in Scotland had been defeated and royal forces were massing in nearby Trowbridge. After being talked out of going once more into exile by his generals, a more than disillusioned Monmouth headed west instead and made his way to Shepton Mallet and Wells before arriving at Bridgwater on 5 July 1685.

The rebel army under the Duke of Monmouth was still around 3,500 strong, but they lay cornered in Bridgwater by a smaller and far more experienced royal army. During the night of the 5/6 July 1685, in a last desperate attempt to salvage something from his abortive rebellion, Monmouth launched a surprise night attack from the least expected direction, across the marshy wastes of Sedgemoor. The rebels' bold strategy was discovered before they reached the royal camp, however, and then, in the darkness, their cavalry failed to locate the ford giving access to the royal camp.

What has become known as the Battle of Sedgemoor was fought in the early morning of the following day – 6 July 1685 – at the site of nearby Westonzoyland, but with the element of surprise lost, any chance of victory had disappeared. The rebel horses soon fled the field and in open country without cavalry support Monmouth's infantry proved an easy target for the royal cavalry. The discipline, experience and firepower of the well-equipped professional soldiers of James II's army soon began to tell. As the morning light revealed the true plight of the rebels, Feversham launched a joint cavalry and infantry attack and Monmouth's army was destroyed.

Monmouth initially escaped but was later captured and executed – the same fate that was to befall many of his followers. More than 1,400 of Monmouth's men were captured and the treason trials, known now as the Bloody Assizes, began in Winchester in August 1685, under the infamous Lord Chief Justice George Jeffreys (Judge Jefferies himself would become known as the 'Hanging Judge'). He then 'toured' the West Country, like some circus horror show. When the trials reached Taunton they were held in the Great Hall, and before it had finished around 300 men were hanged and more than 800 transported to the West Indies.

The tiny village of **Westonzoyland** (www.visitsomerset.co.uk/explore-somerset/westonzoyland) is located about five miles from Bridgwater, and its historical **Pumping Station Museum** (www.wzlet.org) which can be found in Hoopers Lane. It was constructed in 1830 and was the earliest steam powered pumping station to be built – the first of several similar stations on the Somerset Levels. The station is now a small museum, displaying stationary steam engines and exhibits of land drainage history. The pride of the museum, however, is the station's pumping engine which remains in the main engine house; this was built in 1861 to replace an earlier engine that had been pumping since 1831 and is the only one still in its original location and in working order. Other exhibits in the museum include such items as a Wills engine, Lancashire boiler, the original forge and a Lister diesel generating plant. The museum displays several other steam engines and pumps along with a short length of narrow-gauge railway.

Despite the importance of the pumping station, the village lays claim to a much more significant historical event. Although it is known as the Battle of Sedgemoor, the actual defeat of the Duke of Monmouth's rebel force took place at Westonzoyland, and to mark this event there is the Battle of Sedgemoor Memorial. The monument consists of a rough-hewn stone with plaque attached mounted on a two-stepped stone base. There are four inscribed staddle stones at each corner of the base. The main inscription reads:

To the glory of God and in memory of all those who doing the right as they gave it fell in the battle of Sedgemoor 6th July 1685 and lie buried in this field or who, for their share in the fight suffered death, punishment or transportation. PRO PATRIA

Sedgemoor Memorial. © Rog Frost (cc-by-sa/2.0)

Lying on the south side of the Polden Hills about four miles north-east of Bridgwater is the pretty village of **Bawdrip** (www.bawdrip.org.uk) which is notable for the fourteenth-century church of **St Michael & All Angels** and a tablet behind the church altar to which is attached the most tragic story.

> Edward Lovell married Eleanor Bradford, by who he had two daughters, Eleanor and Mary. Eleanor, the daughter, heiress of the family honour and estate, died June 14, 1681. Her most sorrowing husband mourned her, taken away by a sudden and untimely fate at the very time of her marriage celebration, and wished this monument to be put up.

On her wedding day in 1681, so the story goes, a young bride played a game of hide and seek. In the course of this, she hid inside an ancient chest, in a distant and little used part of the house. Its spring lock shut firmly behind her and she was imprisoned, unable to force open the lid, her screams went unheard and her body was not discovered until many years later and the mystery of her wedding-day disappearance solved. Her sad demise has long been believed to have occurred in the Rectory.

Tradition associates the tragic death of Eleanor Lovell with the woeful ballad 'The Mistletoe Bough', compiled sometime after 1820 by Thomas Haynes Bayly, son of a Bath solicitor. Bayly was born in 1797 and lived until 1839. His ballad, based in medieval times, was composed of the happenings and stories gleaned in his own lifetime and cannot be related to historical fact. The song proved very popular and in 1859, its 'solemn chanting' was referred to as a 'national occurrence at Christmas' in English households; by 1862 the song was referred to as 'one of the most popular ever written … which must be known by heart by many readers'. The story has also been linked to Knowle Manor and was at one time the residence of Cromwell's General-at-Sea, Admiral Robert Blake. The tale has been associated with other sites, but a chest that was once kept in the church is claimed to be the very one.

If we now go back towards Bridgwater and then head west, on a circular route around the edge of the district, the first point of call will be **Halswell House.** (www.halswellparktrust.org.uk/halswellhistory). This Grade I listed

Bawdrip Church © Derek Harper (cc-by-sa/2.0)

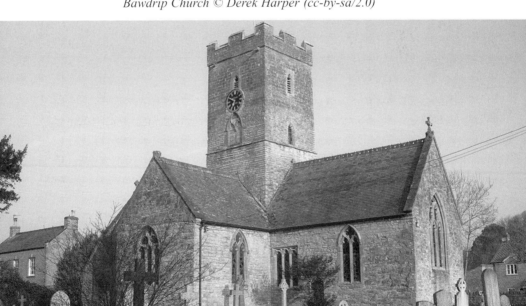

building is located at **Goathurst**, near Bridgwater, and was once part of a great estate. The story of its destruction is typical of so many great houses during the twentieth century: woods were cut down, the deer park put to the plough, and follies collapsed or destroyed. What saved the house itself though was its size, strength and excellent condition. The partial conversion into flats saved it from the wrecking ball and it was restored as one house again in recent times. The eighteenth century pleasure garden, **Mill Wood**, recently came back into estate ownership and the long road to full restoration of all the buildings is now well under way. Because of the continuing renovation works the house is not open to individual visitors all the time, but people can book places on certain tour dates by appointment.

In the 17-acre pleasure garden of Mill Wood stands the **Temple of Harmony** an eighteenth-century folly built in 1767 as a replica of the first-century Temple of Fortuna Virilis in Rome. It was built for Sir Charles Kemeys-Tynte in 1767 to designs by Thomas Prowse, with features by Robert Adam and Thomas Stocking. The Temple was dedicated to the memory of a former MP for Oxford University, Peregrine Palmer, who died in 1762. The Temple has a slate roof and pedimented end gables and is surrounded with Ionic columns and pilasters. It is aligned north-west/ south-east, with the portico at the south-east end, facing Halswell House which lies about 500 yards away. The Somerset Buildings Preservation Trust acquired the derelict Temple in 1993 and after being used as a cattle shelter for many years it has been restored and is a Grade II listed building. John Walsh's marble statue of Terpsichore, the Muse of Joy, which was dedicated to the memory of Thomas Prowse after his death in 1767, has been replaced by a copy, with the original in Taunton's Museum of Somerset for safe keeping. The Temple is owned and managed by the Halswell Park Trust and is occasionally opened to the public.

Nearby is the small village of **Spaxton** (www.spaxton.org.uk) located in the Quantock Hills, and about four miles from Bridgeport. Although it has seldom troubled the historical record, in the mid-nineteenth century it became notorious as home to a religious group known as the **Agapemonite Community** (pronounced Aga-pem-an-ite) otherwise known as the 'Abode of Love'. The Reverend Henry James Prince (1811–99) studied medicine at Guy's Hospital and, having qualified in 1832, was appointed medical officer to the General Hospital in Bath, his native city. He was unable to continue the appointment due to ill health and became curate of Charlinch. Although it had a somewhat small congregation on his appointment, attendances at the church greatly improved when he began to act as if possessed, throwing himself around and adopting practices not wholly in accordance with the established church. In a short time, Prince claimed to have built up a following of about 500 – who gave him everything they owned. The group moved to Spaxton, where Prince declared himself to be the Holy Spirit and announced the world would end shortly. He adopted the policy of arranging spiritual wives among the congregation, which didn't go down well with all his followers – and neither did him having sex with a young virgin in public on a billiard table in the chapel. Henry Prince died in 1911 and it was assumed that his church would die with him, but a man named John Smyth-Piggot, a former sailor, took over and the sect continued until the last adherent died in 1956, whereupon the assets were sold and given to charity. Their 'church' is today a private home.

The Agapemone Today. © Derek Harper (cc-by-sa/2.0)

Another person to cause controversy during his lifetime was Andrew Crosse, a pioneering nineteenth-century electrician who conducted a series of electrical experiments – including the development of large voltaic piles – in his home at **Fyne Court** (www.nationaltrust.org.uk/fyne-court) situated in the village of Broomfield. Having lost both his parents by the time he reached the age of 21, he took over the management of his inherited family estates and began his experiments. Crosse erected 'an extensive apparatus for examining the electricity of the atmosphere', incorporating at one point an insulated wire some 1.25 miles long, later shortened to 1,800ft, which was suspended from poles and trees. Using this wire, he was able to determine the polarity of the atmosphere under various weather conditions. His results were published by his friend George Singer in 1814, as part of Singer's *Elements of Electricity and Electro-Chemistry*.

Along with Sir Humphry Davy, who visited Fyne Court in 1827, Crosse was one of the first to develop large voltaic piles. Noad's *Manual of Electricity* describes a battery consisting of fifty jars containing 73 square ft of coated surface. Using his wires Crosse was able to charge and discharge it some twenty times a minute, 'accompanied by reports almost as loud as those of a cannon', giving rise to him being known locally as 'the thunder and lightning man'. In 1836 Sir Richard Phillips described seeing a wide variety of voltaic piles at Fyne Court, totalling 2,500, of which 1,500 were in use when he was there.

The main building of the court burned down in 1894 and the buildings which survived the fire have been used as offices and a visitor's centre by organisations such as the Somerset Wildlife Trust and Quantock Hills AONB Service, since it came into the ownership of the National Trust in 1967. It is surrounded by a large country estate of woodland, ponds and meadows, while within the original pleasure grounds are a folly and boathouse. It is said that Andrew Crosse's experiments was one of the main influences on Mary Shelley's masterpiece, *Frankenstein*.

Carrying on in the circular direction, another piece of literary history is soon reached. About nine miles from Bridgwater, along the A39, at 35 Lime Street, **Nether Stowey**, lies **Coleridge Cottage** which is now a National Trust property (www.nationaltrust.org.uk/coleridge-cottage). The poet Samuel Taylor Coleridge and his young family rented this seventeenth-century building for three years from 1797. During Coleridge's time at the house, Wordsworth visited him and subsequently rented Alfoxton Park, a little over three miles away. There are references to the cottage in several of Coleridge's poems, including 'To The Rev G Coleridge' (lines 52–61), 'This Lime Tree Bower My Prison'; 'Frost at Midnight'; and 'Fears in Solitude' (lines 221–226).

The cottage was refurbished in 1800 and run as an inn. Major work took place in the second-half of the nineteenth century, when rooms were added at the back of the building and the roof was raised. In 1893, a committee of Coleridge's admirers took a lease on the property for fifteen years at £15 per annum, and by 1896 an appeal had been launched to raise more money for the lease or eventual purchase, with the threat that it could be removed to America. They installed a commemorative plaque on the wall, which was unveiled on 9 June 1893, and by 1908 the campaign, chaired by the Earl of Lytton, had gained much public support including that of archbishops of Canterbury and York, and raised the funds needed to purchase the property.

As for **Alfoxton House** itself, which is also known as Alfoxton Park, this is an eighteenth-century country house that was rebuilt after the original was destroyed by fire in 1710. It is in the village of Holford, which is around ten miles west of Bridgwater and like Nether Stowey, set within the Quantock Hills. William Wordsworth and his sister Dorothy lived here between July 1797 and June 1798, to be near their new friend, Coleridge. Dorothy began her famous journals here, although she discontinued them after a couple of months, not to begin them again until she and her brother were safely ensconced in the Lake District. The house has been designated by English Heritage as Grade II listed and during the Second World War, housed evacuees from a school in Kent.

Heading northward now, the coast is soon reached, and it is here that we find **Burnham-on-Sea** (www.burnham-on-sea.com). This is a large seaside town located at the mouth of the River Parrett, next to Bridgwater Bay, which grew from a small fishing village in the late eighteenth century to become a popular seaside resort. The position of the town on the edge of the Somerset Levels and moors, where they meet the Bristol Channel, has resulted in a history dominated by land reclamation and sea defences ever since the time of the Romans. Burnham was seriously affected by the Bristol Channel floods of 1607, and modern sea defences have been put in place with the present curved concrete wall having been completed in 1988. There have been many shipwrecks on the Gore Sands, which lie just off-shore and their remains can sometimes be exposed at low tides. Lighthouses are prominent landmarks in the town, with the original, known as the Round Tower, built to replace the light on the top of the fourteenth century tower of St Andrews Church. The Esplanade along the sea front contains several listed buildings from the early nineteenth century, and on the corner of Berrow Road and Sea View, is a **drinking fountain** from 1897, with a single dressed-stone pier and moulded plinth, topped by a cast iron urn. Each side has the lion's head design, with those on the north and south sides giving water into a Purbeck Marble bowl.

Brent Knoll Camp (www.brentknollvillage.co.uk) a couple of miles from Burnham-on-Sea, is an Iron Age hillfort and ancient monument in the care of the National Trust who acquired the freehold of 33 acres in 1979. The hill is 449ft high and dominates the low surrounding landscape of the Somerset Levels and is visible from the M5. The word 'knoll' usually means a small hill or hill-top. Before the Somerset Levels were drained, Brent Knoll was an island, known as the Isle (or Mount) of Frogs, that provided a haven from the water and marshes. It became an island once more during the Bristol Channel floods of 1607.

The site has seen human settlement since at least the Bronze Age, becoming an Iron Age Fort in about 2000 BC. It covers an area of 4 acres and is defended by a single wall around 33ft high with a single ditch and an entrance on the eastern side, with a second bank on the north east side. It is surrounded by multiple ramparts (multivallate) which follow the contours of the hill, now heavily damaged by cattle and quarrying.

The Romans used its summit as a fortification and an urn containing coins of the Roman Emperors Trajan and Severus was found at the site in the late eighteenth century. Other finds have included pennant sandstone roof tiles and painted wall plaster, indicative of a substantial building which is more likely to have been a temple than a villa. Many of the finds are in the Somerset County and Weston-super-Mare Museums, with Romano-British pottery in the Blake Museum, Bridgwater.

The fort has been claimed as the site of Mons Badonicus, a legendary battle between a force of Britons and an Anglo-Saxon army, which probably took place sometime between AD 490 and 517. Though it is believed to have been a major political and military event, there is no certainty about its date or location. It is also believed to have been the site of a battle in 875 at which forces of the Anglo-Saxon kingdom of Wessex drove away the Great Heathen Army led by Guthrum, prior to the Treaty of Wedmore, which was signed three years later. During the medieval era the local land was held by Glastonbury Abbey until the dissolution of the monasteries in 1536. Around the sides and top of the hill are several scarps which may be medieval strip lynchets. In 2006 a resistivity survey undertaken at the northern end of the hill fort showed several linear features that may have been structures.

Limestone was quarried from the knoll, possibly during the nineteenth century, and during the Second World War it was the site of a gun emplacement manned by the Home Guard. The remains of slit trenches with angle-iron stakes can still be seen on the western and south-western sides. A stone marker on the hill, which also serves as a triangulation station, commemorates the golden jubilee of Queen Victoria.

Brent Knoll © william (cc-by-sa/2.0)

St Michael's Church is worth a visit as it contains some Norman work as well as a wagon-style roof with some fourteenth-century bosses and stone heads. The tower is 75ft high and built in the early fifteenth century. The memorial chapel commemorates the villagers who fell in the Second World War and in the churchyard there is a war memorial erected in 1920 which now bears the names of those who died in both world wars.

Carrying on in a somewhat circular direction, we next find the **Isle of Wedmore** (www.theisleofwedmore.net) the home of cider producer **Roger Wilkins Cider Farm** (wilkinscider.com) which occupies Land's End Farm at Mudgley. The farmhouse contains a nineteenth-century press that is still used today, and the walls are covered with photographs and cuttings, including a yellowing page from an old *Q Magazine* containing an interview with the late Clash singer, Joe Strummer. Encircled is his description of happiness: 'Chilling in Somerset with a flagon of Wilkins Farmhouse Cider.' The rock star connection doesn't stop there though: Chris Jagger, brother of Rolling Stone Mick, lives next door. 'Johnny Rotten, Nick Cave, Dave Gilmour – they all come here,' or so Rogers' says.

Leaving Wedmore behind, our route soon reaches the small town of **Axbridge** (www.visitsomerset.co.uk/explore-somerset/axbridge) and the **King John's Hunting Lodge** (www.kingjohnshuntinglodge.co.uk) which was a wool-merchant's house built in around 1460. The building consists of a jettied timber-frame occupying a corner plot on the town square. The house is the finest of several timber-framed houses that lie in the High Street and The Square. The three-storey building is jettied on two adjacent sides and has three gables on the longer side. On the first and second floors, curved brackets can be seen supporting the floor above. The structure is based around a single wooden post, known as a king post, at the front corner of the building, which supports the floor boards and the horizontal dragon beams that carry the projection of the upper floors at each level. In 1340 the site was occupied by shops on the ground floor, living areas and workshops on the first floor, and storage and sleeping areas on the second floor when it was known as 'the stockhouse'. The current building has served a variety of purposes and at one time part of it became The King's Head Inn.

The origin of its present name is unclear as it was not built until long after the reign of King John, who died in 1216. The hunting lodge name first appeared in a 1915 publication, *The Heart of Mendip* by Francis Knight, when it was being run as a saddler's shop. The royal part of the name may have come from the fact that there was a carved king's head on the building, from a time when it was used as a public house but whether this represented King John, or another king is not known. The head was attached to one corner of the exterior, but is now inside the building, and a replica placed on the outside. In the nineteenth and early twentieth centuries, the building housed a succession of shops and underwent various changes which contributed to its physical decline. A Miss Ripley bought the building in 1930 and used it to store her collection of antiques until 1968, allowing the public to see her collection once a year. She bequeathed it to the National Trust who undertook the works necessary to make it fit for visitors and saved it from probable destruction.

In overhauling the structure of the premises, the National Trust restored its medieval character by recreating the appearance of arcaded stalls

King John's Hunting Lodge, Axbridge. © Richard Croft (cc-by-sa/2.0)

opening onto the street on the ground floor, and the sixteenth-century decoration of the upstairs windows, although this caused some controversy as it required the removal of some fine eighteenth-century windows. The Grade II listed building is now leased to **Axbridge and District Museum** who operate it as a local museum which includes exhibits relating to local geology and history from the Neolithic era to the Second World War

About five miles from Axbridge, at Chapel Allerton, lies the **Ashton Windmill,** a tower mill dating from the eighteenth century which was modernised in 1900 with machinery brought from the demolished Moorlinch Mill. Iron hoops were added around the building to give it some support and it was further restored in 1967. The mill was given to Bristol City Museum in 1966 and is owned by Sedgemoor District Council

Next on this circular itinerary, and not far down the road from Axbridge, is **Cheddar Gorge** (www.cheddargorge.co.uk) named as the second greatest natural wonder in Britain, surpassed only by the Dan yr Ogof caves. The Gorge itself attracts about 500,000 visitors a year and is a spectacular sight at about 450ft deep, with a near vertical cliff face to the south and steep grassy slopes to the north; the B3135 runs along its bottom. A wide variety of wild birds may be seen here including peregrine falcons, buzzards, kestrels, ravens and the grasshopper warbler. This world-famous beauty spot includes the **Cheddar Man Museum of Prehistory,** which contains information about the caves and their palaeontological development. The exhibits include original flint tools and replicas of the human remains excavated from the caves.

Gough's Cave is 377ft deep and nearly 3½ miles long and contains a variety of large chambers and rock formations including the Cheddar Yeo, the largest underground river system in Britain. The first 2,690ft of the cave are open to the public as a show cave, and this stretch contains most of the more spectacular formations. The greater part of the cave's length is made up of the river passage, which is accessible only by diving.

The initial sections, previously known as Sand Hole, were accessible before the nineteenth century; between 1892 and 1898 Richard Cox Gough, who lived in Lion House nearby, found, excavated and opened to the public, further areas of the cave, up to Diamond Chamber, which is the end of the show cave today. Electric lighting was installed in the show caves as early as 1899. The cave is subject to flooding which often lasts up to forty-eight hours, however in the Great Flood of 1968 this lasted for three days. The extensive, flooded parts of the cave system were found and explored between 1985 and 1990.

When excavated, the cave was found to contain skeletal remains of both humans and animals, all showing cut-marks and breakages which a technique known as 3D microscopy showed to be consistent with de-fleshing, similar to the way in which animal carcasses had been prepared for food. Although this is quite possibly evidence of cannibalism, it is by no means certain and any number of ritual practices may account for it. Chris Stringer of the Natural History Museum, one of the world experts on such things, favours the cannibalism theory. Skull fragments discovered represented from five to seven humans, including a young child of about 3 years and two adolescents. The brain cases appear to have been prepared as drinking cups or containers, a tradition found in other Magdalenian sites across Europe and again there are many possible reasons for this, from mere practicality to respect for the ancestors or contempt for their enemies. In 2010 the human bones were subject to further examination and some were dated to around the end of the Ice Age, an amazing 14,700 years ago.

In 1903 the remains of a human male, since named **Cheddar Man**, were found a short distance inside Gough's Cave. His is Britain's oldest complete human skeleton, having been dated to approximately 7,150 years BC. There is a suggestion that the man died a violent death. Mitochondrial DNA taken from the skeleton has been found to match that of Adrian Targett, a retired history teacher living in the local area in 2018, indicating that Cheddar Man is a very distant relative. Further genome sequencing indicated that he was most likely to have had blue eyes and a 'very dark brown to black complexion and dark curly hair'. However, a subsequent report in *New Scientist* announced some scepticism from within the scientific community regarding the findings. The remains are in the Natural History Museum in London, with a replica in the *Cheddar Man and the Cannibals Museum* in the Gorge. Other human remains have also been found in the cave and in 2007 a carving of a mammoth, estimated to be 13,000 years old, was also found there.

Cheddar Caves. © Eugene Birchall (cc-by-sa/2.0)

Food and Drink

Gardeners Arms, 35 Silver Street, Cheddar, BS27 3LE. 01934 741 472 – A restaurant and pub in the quiet roads in the old part of Cheddar, 300 yards away from the Gorge. Parts of the building date back to the time of Queen Elizabeth. The bar area is plushily carpeted with high-back seats and wrought iron tables. The menu consists mainly of homemade dishes with emphasis on fish and exotic meat dishes. Food is served in either the bar or restaurant area, while in good weather dining is catered for in the gardens, with a great view of Cheddar Gorge.

Cobblestones, 71 Eastover, Bridgwater, TA6 5AP. 01278 429 865 – This friendly pub has a courtyard garden to the rear and a function room which hosts live rock bands. Pub quizzes and pub sports also feature. In addition to four ales there is a strong commitment to real cider from polypins. Between the town centre and the railway station.

Fountain Inn, 1 West Quay, Bridgwater, TA6 3HL. 01278 444 951 – Recently refurbished town centre, single-room traditional pub, with wood-burning stove. Free house next to the River Parrett and the historic town bridge. Three regular ales, Butcombe Bitter, Moles Rucking Mole and Dark.

King Alfred Inn, Burrow Drove, Burrowbridge, TA7 0RB. 01823 698 379 – A welcoming old-fashioned free house on the Somerset Levels between Taunton and Bridgwater. Positioned under the shadow of Burrow Mump, where King Alfred is supposed to have burned the cakes. A perfect stopping-off point for walkers on the River Parrett Trail. Good locally sourced seasonal food all sessions except Sunday evening, including excellent weekday hearty lunches. Friday fish supper is deservedly popular – www.kingalfredinn.com.

Sedgemoor Inn, 19 Main Road, Westonzoyland, TA7 0EB. 01278 691 382 – This is a traditional country pub where you can enjoy freshly prepared food Tuesday–Sunday, from light-bites, pub classics or something from the grill. The pub frontage has a mural depicting the battle of Sedgemoor – www.sedgemoorinnwestonzoyland.co.uk

Dunstan House Inn, 8-10 Love Lane, Burnham-on-Sea, TA8 1EU. 01278 784 343 – Large Young's pub next to the hospital with a flagstone floor in the bar area, a raised dining area, a family room and two open log fires. Outside there is covered decking, garden and children's play equipment. Daily specials enhance the food menu which includes a children's menu and Sunday roast. Quiz night held on a Wednesday. En-suite accommodation is available – www.dunstanhouseinn.co.uk.

The Lamb, The Square, Axbridge, BS26 2AP. 01934 732 253 – Lovely Grade II listed Butcombe-owned coaching house in the village square opposite the Hunting lodge where 'Hanging Judge Jeffreys' held court. There is a large low-beamed bar area and several smaller, quieter areas leading off it. Outside drinking spaces are to the front and rear via the courtyard. Wholesome and interesting meals are served, with daily offers for Butcombe loyalty-card holders. Thatchers and Navelgazer ciders are usually on together with a bag-in-box selection. Bar skittles, pool and darts. The Weston to Wells 26 and 126 buses stop nearby during the day – www.butcombe.com/pubs/the-lamb-hotel

CHAPTER 4

South Somerset

If you're heading into the South Somerset district from the previous one, then the most direct route is to follow the A372 from Bridgwater, and through Westonzoyland. By travelling on this road, it brings you to the town of **Langport**. During the First English Civil War, the Battle of Langport took place on 10 July 1645 (www.sommilmuseum.org.uk/battle-of-langport). The outcome was a decisive Parliamentary victory,

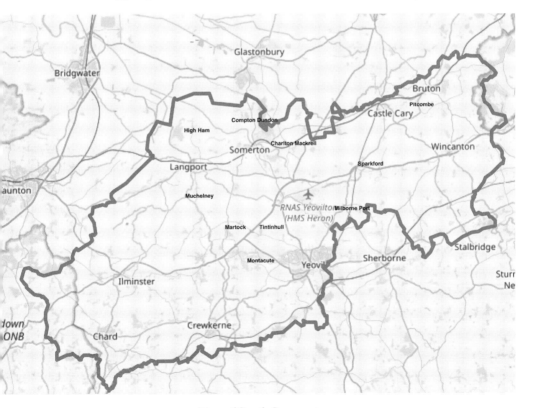

Map of South Somerset.

and as the Royalists fled, they left most of their equipment behind. Situated by Bow Bridge over the River Parrett, the **Langport Visitors' Centre** has displays and exhibitions related to the local past, industry and the natural history of the river. It is a central point for information about the River Parrett Trail, a long-distance footpath that follows the route of the River Parrett. The trail, which is fifty miles long, runs from Chedington in Dorset to the mouth of the river in Bridgwater Bay, where it joins the West Somerset Coast Path.

Muchelney Abbey, in the village of Muchelney, is less than two miles from Langport (www.english-heritage.org.uk/visit/places/muchelney-abbey) and was once effectively an island within a marshy and frequently flooded area. The site today consists of the **Abbot's House** and ruined walls showing the layout of the abbey buildings constructed between the seventh to sixteenth centuries. The abbey was damaged by Viking raids and rebuilt in the tenth century, then expanded from the twelfth to sixteenth centuries. During the time of the Domesday book, in 1086, the abbey paid a tax of 6,000 eels a year, caught from the local rivers and marshes. Much of the abbey was rebuilt under abbots William Wyke and Thomas Broke.

The whole property was granted to Edward Seymour, Earl of Hertford, later 1st Duke of Somerset, and on his execution in 1552 it reverted to the crown. By the sixteenth century the abbey included an abbey church, the demesne farm, an almonry, the parish church of St Peter and St Paul with its vicarage, and a cross dating from the fifteenth century (moved in 1830 to near the parish church). The monastic church was built on the site of an early Saxon church. In the inquiry into monastic finances of 1535, Muchelney was recorded as distributing £6 13s 4d in cash as alms. In 1538 the abbey, with all land and possessions, was surrendered by the monks to Henry VIII in the course of the dissolution of the monasteries. The main buildings of the abbey were then demolished, some of the decorative floor tiles were re-laid in the neighbouring Church of St Peter and St Paul and some of the stone was used in many local buildings – in 1872 when collecting stone, labourers found a blue stone coffin lid under which the pavement of the fourteenth century lady chapel. In 1927 the ruins of the abbey were taken over by the Office of Works, which became English Heritage and is a listed building.

Muchelney Abbey. © Paul Farmer (cc-by-sa/2.0)

The **Priest's House**, as its name would suggest, was built by the abbey in 1308 for the parish priest and incorporates gothic doorway, tracery windows and fifteenth-century fireplace. By 1608 the building was said to be 'ruinous', but was used by the vicar or curate until around 1840, when it served as a cellar and later as a school, before being rented to a farmer in the late nineteenth century. It was acquired by the National Trust in 1911 and is leased to a tenant who provides limited access to the public.

The **Church of St Peter & St Paul** in Law Lane is well worth a visit if only for its vaulted ceiling with panels covered with extraordinary multi-coloured paintings depicting clouds, cherubs and angels in various states of undress, some of them bare-breasted. The figures date from the seventeenth century and are thought to symbolise purity, but it is quite remarkable that they survived without being whitewashed over by the Puritans or Victorians. It could almost be thought that they were offering a two-fingered salute to the clergy far below!

The last remaining thatched windmill in England is **Stembridge Windmill** at High Ham, five miles to the north of Langport; it is the sole

Angels at St Peter & St Paul, © Michael Garlick (cc-by-sa/2.0)

survivor of five windmills that once existed in the area. Constructed in 1822, the mill has been designated a Grade II listed building and is owned by the National Trust. In 2009 it underwent a £100,000 restoration by local craftsmen funded by the Grantscape Community Heritage Fund and reopened later that year.

From here, find your way back onto the B3153 and then head east towards **Somerton** (www.visitsomerset.co.uk/explore-somerset). As might be inferred, it gave its name to the county; it may have been the capital of Wessex in the tenth. Its history dates as far back as the Anglo-Saxon period, when it was a significant political and commercial centre. The importance of the town declined following the Norman conquest despite it being the county town of Somerset in the late thirteenth and early fourteenth century. Having lost this status, Somerton became a thriving market town in the Middle Ages, whose economy was supported by transport systems which

Stembridge Windmill. © Martin Bodman (cc-by-sa/2.0)

used the River Parrett, and later rail via the Great Western Railway, along with light industries including glove-making and gypsum-mining.

In the centre of town the wide market square, with its octagonal-roofed market cross, is surrounded by old houses, while close by is the thirteenth-century Church of St Michael and All Angels. Somerton also had links with Muchelney Abbey in the Middle Ages.

National Trust

The National Trust for Places of Historic Interest or Natural Beauty, commonly known simply as the **National Trust**, is an independent charity and membership organisation for environmental and heritage conservation in England, Wales and Northern Ireland. The trust was founded on 12 January 1895 by Octavia Hill (1838–1912), Sir Robert Hunter (1844–1913) and Hardwicke Rawnsley (1851–1920), prompted in part by the earlier success of Charles Eliot and the Kyrle Society. Over the years the Trust has been given statutory powers, starting with the National Trust Act 1907. In the early days, the trust was concerned primarily with protecting open spaces and a variety of threatened buildings – the trust describes itself as 'a charity that works to preserve and protect historic places and spaces – for ever, for everyone'.

Historically, the trust tended to focus on English country houses, which still make up the largest part of its holdings, but it also protects historic landscapes such as in the Lake District, historic urban properties, and nature reserves. The focus on country houses and gardens came about in the mid-twentieth century when the private owners of many of the properties were no longer able to afford to maintain them. Many were donated to the trust in lieu of death duties.

The Trust, one of the largest UK charities financially, is funded by membership subscriptions, entrance fees, legacies, and revenue from gift shops and restaurants within its properties. It has been accused of focusing too much on country estates, and in recent years, the trust has sought to broaden its activities by acquiring historic properties such as former mills, early factories, workhouses, and the childhood homes of Paul McCartney and John Lennon.

The National Trust has been the beneficiary of many large donations and bequests. It owns over 350 heritage properties, which includes many historic houses and gardens, industrial monuments, and social history sites. Most of these are open to the public, usually for a charge. Others are leased, on terms that manage to preserve their character. The Trust is one of the largest landowners in the United Kingdom, owning over 247,000 hectares (610,000 acres; 2,470 km^2; 950 square miles) of land, including many characteristic sites of natural beauty, most of which are open to the public free of charge – www.nationaltrust.org.uk

The Market has had a cross in the square since before 1390; the present **Butter Cross**, a roofed market cross, was rebuilt in 1673 and is Somerton's most noted feature. The structure was the property of the Earls of Ilchester who sold it to the town in 1916. Next to the Butter Cross stands the '**Market Hall**', previously known as the 'Town Hall', although the building has never fulfilled either of these functions. Bordering the square are the church, and the Lady Smith Memorial Hall, also known as the 'Parish Rooms', which was built in 1902, and the seventeenth-century Market House, now a restaurant. The Red Lion was opened by the Earl of Ilchester in 1768 as a model coaching inn. It closed in 1995 and after a period of neglect, has been redeveloped as town houses. From the early 1980s onwards projects have been undertaken that aim to improve Somerton for film-industry purposes. The market square was extensively remodelled, creating a central parking area with easy access to the local amenities.

Somerton Court, at Lower Somerton was originally known as 'Somerton Erleigh' and has had various owners including Edward IV's brother, the Duke of Clarence, and Henry Percy, 6th Earl of Northumberland, who sold the estate in 1530. It passed through several hands until 1597 when it was purchased by James Fisher, whose son later rebuilt it in 1641. The court remained in the Fisher family's possession until 1808 when it was sold and renamed 'Somerton Court' by its new owners, who replaced the gabled dormers with Gothic battlements and turrets. The house was later enlarged by the Hall-Stephenson family, was occupied by WRNS personnel during the Second World War, and was purchased by a local businessman,

Lytes Cary Manor [Photo © Sarah Charlesworth (cc-by-sa/2.0)].

Stuart Pattemore, in the 1970s. In 1987 the house and estate of 55 acres and four cottages, including The Dower House, built in the early nineteenth century, was purchased by Roger Byron-Collins when it was subjected to extensive upgrading and extensions. It was resold in 2005.

About five miles further east from Somerton is **Lytes Cary Manor** (www.nationaltrust.org.uk/lytes-cary-manor). This is a picturesque fifteenth-century house set in a glorious garden near the village of Charlton Mackrell. The manor was the birthplace and home of the Elizabethan herbalist Henry Lyte, whose 1578 compendium *Lyte's Herbal* was one of the most influential books on the natural world ever printed. The surrounding garden borders are based on the illustrations of this volume. The property is now owned by the National Trust, is Grade I listed and has parts dating from the fourteenth through to the twentieth century. The chapel predates the existing house, and functioned as a chantry chapel, where masses could be said for the souls of the family, living and dead. The gardens are Grade II listed.

Now return to Somerton, take the B3165 south and after crossing the A372, continue until you reach **Martock Treasurers House**. This is a hamstone-built medieval priest's house from the thirteenth century, with various extensions and alterations since. The Great Hall was completed in 1293, but there is an earlier solar block with an interesting wall painting. The building is a Grade I listed and operated by the National Trust.

Five miles to the north east of Yeovil, towering 500ft above sea level, is **Cadbury Castle** (www.sommilmuseum.org.uk), a large hill with a summit which encompasses about 18 acres. The hill has been occupied since Neolithic times and bones found there have been radiocarbon-dated to 3500 BC, but the main period of occupation was during the Iron Age when the large hillfort was constructed. Its position and the size of its ramparts are definite indications of a military purpose. Excavations in the late 1960s revealed elaborate timber defences on top of the ramparts and indications of domestic buildings within. The castle or camp was the site of a violent battle between the British tribes and the invading Romans during the period of invasion. There are indications that a Romano-British Temple once occupied part of the site and after the Romans withdrew, the Saxons constructed a Great Hall, measuring 66ft by 33ft. Romantics have linked the site to the mythical King Arthur and suggested that this may have been the site of his palace of Camelot.

Not far away are two more properties operated by the National Trust. The first is one of the most beautiful country houses in the county. **Montacute House** (www.nationaltrust.org.uk/montacute-house) stands just off the A3088, about five miles from Yeovil, and has the unassuming address of 17 Middle Street. It was built by the Phelips family, who rose in status from yeoman farmers to become knights and Parliamentarians; while another of them, Edward, was a lawyer who became chief prosecutor against the gunpowder plotters of 1605. The 'E plan' manor dates from the 1590s and is built in the English Renaissance style; the main façade has Dutch gables decorated with clambering stone monkeys and other animals. On the ground floor was the great hall, kitchens and pantries, on the upper floors, retiring rooms for the family and honoured guests. Initially, the large hall would have been the most important communal eating and living room, but by the time the house was completed, this traditional area was largely an anachronism. Over the centuries, the layout and use of rooms changed and drawing and dining rooms evolved on the ground floor. In keeping with most buildings of the time, Montacute had no corridors, with one room leading directly to another. One of its most unusual features is a long plaster frieze in the hall depicting a 'Skimmington ride', which was an ancient form of public humiliation. On this occasion the frieze depicts a husband whose wife catches him having a drink when he should have been looking after the baby. She hits him on the head with a shoe and the locals parade him around the village astride a pole to be ridiculed. Outside, there are around 260 acres of parkland and 10 acres of more formal gardens.

Four miles away from Montacute lies yet another important historical estate, that of **Tintinhull House & Gardens** (www.nationaltrust.org.uk/tintinhull-garden), which lies in Farm Street within the quaint village of Tintinhull. The house is Grade I listed and although in private hands it can be booked for holiday-lets via the National Trust. The gardens are laid out into areas separated by walls and hedges and were developed in the early twentieth century to include triangular and diamond shaped flagstone paths. The early landscaping was expanded and planted starting in 1933 by Phyllis Reiss in an Arts and Crafts 'Hidcote' style. The garden is separated into 'rooms' by yew hedges and walls. The different areas include Eagle Court (the former courtyard), Middle Garden, Fountain Garden and Pool Garden. The pool garden is the site of a former tennis court.

Also nearby is the collection that makes up the **Museum of South Somerset** (http://southsomersetmuseums.org.uk). Located at 7 Artillery Road, Lufton, it was started by Alderman W.R.E. Mitchelmore, Mayor of Yeovil (1918–1921), and was initially based in the former coach house to Hendford Manor, moving to its present location three miles outside Yeovil in 2011. The collection has an emphasis on local history and includes archaeology, history of the gloving and manufacturing trades, an extensive photography archive, and a firearms collection of international importance.

The main impulse might be to head north from here, and the attractions that lie this way certainly warrant a visit, but the rest of the south and south-east of the section deserve at least a mention.

The market town of **Ilminster** (www.visitilminster.co.uk) is mentioned in historical documents dating from AD 725, as well as within a Charter granted to the Abbey of Muchelney by King Ethelred in AD 995. Ilminster is mentioned in the Domesday Book as Ileminstre, meaning 'The church on the River Isle', from the Old English ysle and mynster. By this period Ilminster was a flourishing community and was granted the right to hold a weekly market, which it still does. In 1645, during the English Civil War, Ilminster was the scene of a skirmish between Parliamentary troops under Edward Massie and Royalist forces under Lord Goring, who fought for control of the bridges prior to the Battle of Langport. The town itself contains the buildings of a sixteenth-century grammar school, the Ilminster Meeting House, which acts as the town's art gallery and concert hall. **Ilchester Museum** is at the town hall and was established in 1989. The museum contains exhibits showing the history of the town from the Iron Age and Roman periods, when it was known as Lindinis, to the present day. They include the town's thirteenth-century mace or staff of office, bearing the insignia of Richard I, which is the oldest staff of office in England. The collection also includes a full set of Maundy Money, acquired in 1995. Five miles from Ilminster is the Tudor manor house of **Barrington Court,** which was covered in an earlier section.

Located in the Market Square, the **Crewkerne & District Museum & Heritage Centre (**www.crewkernemuseum.co.uk) opened in 2000 in an old house with an eighteenth-century frontage. Exhibits cover the development of the town during the eighteenth and nineteenth centuries, with emphasis on the flax and linen industry. Other collections relate to local archaeology, coins and medals, costume and textiles, science and technology, social history, weapons and war.

The town of **Chard** (www.visitsomerset.co.uk/explore-somerset/chard) lies near the Devon border, fifteen miles south west of Yeovil. In 1685 Chard was one of the towns to host some of Judge Jeffreys's Bloody Assizes following the failure of the Monmouth Rebellion. It is home to the Chard canal, built between 1835 and 1842, and the Chard railway branch line created in 1860 to connect the London & South Western Railway and Bristol & Exeter Railway main lines, which ran through the town until 1965. One very unusual feature is a stream running along either side of Fore Street. One stream eventually flows into the Bristol Channel and the other reaches the English Channel.

The sixteenth century thatched **Godworthy House** in the High Street was restored for use as a museum in 1970 (www.chardmuseum.co.uk/

godworthy-house). Its exhibits tell the story of the town and the surrounding locale including geology, the fire of 1577 – during which most of the town was destroyed – the Monmouth Rebellion and local lace mills. Outside there is a blacksmith's forge and display of farm machinery. There are also displays on notable people with connections to the town, such as **John Stringfellow** and **William Samuel Henson,** who achieved the first powered flight in a disused lace factory in 1848, with a 10ft steam-driven flying machine; **James Gillingham,** who was a pioneer of the development of articulated artificial limbs – the museum includes a representation of his consulting room and examples of his artificial limbs; and Victoria Cross recipient **Corporal Samuel Vickery,** who was awarded the medal in 1897 for his actions during the attack on the Dargai Heights, Tirah, India during the Tirah Campaign.

Across the county, on the eastern side of this section is another site worth a visit. The village of **Milborne Port** (www.milborneport.com) would be of interest if only because it is not a port at all and lies far inland; the name 'port' means an important market town. One of its claims to fame, though, comes from a tragi-comic tale from 1770. The case of 'Scott v Shepherd' helped establish the principles of remoteness, foreseeability, and intervening cause in modern personal injury law. A man named Shepherd playfully tossed a lit squib, or firework, into the crowded marketplace, where it landed on the table of a gingerbread-merchant named Yates. Willis, a bystander, grabbed the squib and threw it across the market to protect himself and the gingerbread. Unfortunately, the squib landed in the goods of another merchant named Ryal, who immediately grabbed the squib and tossed it away, accidentally hitting Scott in the face just as the squib exploded. The explosion put out one of Scott's eyes. Shepherd was found to be fully liable, because, said the judge, 'I do not consider [the intermediaries] as free agents in the present case, but acting under a compulsive necessity for their own safety and self-preservation.'

Local features include the nearby **Laycock Railway Cutting,** which is the best single exposure of the Bathonian Fuller's Earth Rock in South Somerset. **Miller's Hill** is a geological site of Special Scientific Interest that is an important and historically famous locality for studies of Middle Jurassic (Bajocian) stratigraphy and palaeontology.

It is now time to head north from Yeovil and the first main attraction is the **Fleet Air Arm Museum** (www.fleetairarm.com) at RNAS Yeovilton, which lies seven miles from Yeovil. It has an extensive collection of military and civilian aircraft, and models of Royal Navy ships, especially aircraft carriers. There are some interactive displays and viewing areas where visitors can watch military aircraft (especially helicopters) take off and land. At the time of writing, there are ninety-four aircraft in the museum's collection.

Making your way onto the A303 and then heading east, brings one to another famous museum: **Haynes Motor Museum** (www. haynesmotormuseum.com). Located at Sparkford, it contains over 400 cars and motorcycles and a collection of other automobilia. It was established in 1985 as an Educational Charitable Trust chaired by John Haynes OBE (1938–2019), of Haynes Publishing Group, the company which publishes the renowned Haynes Manuals.

From Sparkford, off the A359 heading to Bruton, **Castle Cary Museum** (www.castlecarymuseum.org.uk) is housed in the Market House, first erected in 1616 but rebuilt in 1855. There is a varied collection of exhibits; the earliest are local fossils including ammonites, with a display about the discovery of an ichthyosaurus at Alford. Others are on local industry and agriculture and the production of rope and hemp. There are examples of agricultural implements, tools and relics, with an explanation of the local geology. Information is also provided about the town, as well as a room dedicated to the life and work of Parson James Woodforde (1740–1803), who kept diaries detailing rural life in the eighteenth century. The museum is run by volunteers from the Castle Cary and District Museum and Preservation Society. It is also worth a visit to the tiny prison known as the **'Round House'** behind the museum on Bailey Hill built in 1779. The 'blind house', as such lock-ups were called due to the lack of windows, measures only 7ft in diameter and part of that space is taken up with a stone privy, so hopefully not too many of the locals misbehaved at the same time. A resolution was passed in 1785 that all children over the age of 7 who were caught playing when they should have been in Sunday School were to be incarcerated there for a while.

Much of nearby **Gants Mill** at Pitcombe outside Bruton was built in 1810 and includes parts of an eighteenth-century building and possibly some material from earlier mills. Most of the machinery, including grindstones, conveyors, sack hoist and grain bins date from 1888, and is still used for grinding animal feed and occasionally whole wheat flour. South Somerset Hydropower Group was founded in 2001 and the first turbine, at Gants Mill, was commissioned in 2003. The water garden includes seasonal displays of iris, roses, delphiniums, day lilies, clematis, and dahlias.

Bruton Community Museum (www.brutonmuseum.org.uk) at 26 High Street celebrates the history of Bruton and the local area; exhibitions are regularly changed throughout the year (March, July and October), and a free information guide is available at the door. The museum tells

The Top of the Hood Column [Photo © Pam Goodey (cc-by-sa/2.0)].

the story of Bruton's past and present through a plethora of displayed artefacts from the Jurassic, Roman, Saxon and medieval periods, as well as more contemporary displays. Domestic objects, twentieth-century shoes, the unique sculptures of Ernst Blensdorf, a Second World War German refugee, and the writing desk used by the American writer John Steinbeck, who lived in Bruton in 1959, are just some of the highlights.

The final stop in this section is the **Wincanton Museum and History Society** (www.wincantonmuseum.org.uk) which is housed within Wincanton Library, Carrington Way, and has a collection of artefacts, documents, posters and photographs related to the social history of Wincanton and the surrounding district. There is also a replica of a Victorian kitchen and a collection of nineteenth- and twentieth-century farm implements. A separate room is devoted to the First World War and to the Second World War, when American soldiers were stationed in the town prior to the D-Day landings.

Hood Monument

The Hood Monument stands on Windmill Hill at Compton Dundon near Butleigh and dominates the surrounding countryside. It is a memorial to Vice Admiral Sir Samuel Hood who joined the navy in 1776 and two years later took part in his first naval engagement at the Battle of Ushant against the French. He rose through a very distinguished career to become Vice Admiral of the White and fight at the Battle of the Nile, and as Captain of the *Zealous* led the attack at Aboukir Bay which destroyed most of the French fleet and brought about one the greatest English naval sea victories. During a battle off Rochefort in September 1805, he lost his right arm and thus missed taking part in Trafalgar. Hood was promoted to Rear Admiral a few days later, and in 1807 he was put in charge of operations at Madeira, which he brought to a successful conclusion. The following year he was elected a Member of Parliament for Westminster. He died on Christmas Eve 1814 on active service, while Commander-in-Chief of the Indian Station and his body was interred beneath the pavement of the Church of St Mary in Fort George, Madras.

His monument was completed in 1831 to a design by Henry Goodridge and consists of a Tuscan column on an ashlar base set on two tall steps; the lower one supporting a wrought-iron railing enclosure. The whole structure reaches a height of 110ft and its proportions were based on those of Trajan's column in Rome. The monument culminates in a band of laurel wreaths beneath a naval crown, composed of the sculpted sterns of four galleons interspersed with four mainsails. It was carved by Gahagan of Bath and paid for by public subscription. It was originally linked to the Hood family home at Butleigh through a mile-long avenue of cedar trees. The inscription was composed by Sir James Mackintosh. There was originally a doorway in the base, but this was sealed in 1990.

At the opening ceremony in 1831, however, tragedy struck. Veterans were charged with firing a cannon in a royal salute, as part of the celebrations, and Edmund Lye, a Butleigh resident who had fought at the Battle of Waterloo, was ramming the cartridge down into the gun when it exploded. As a contemporary report says,

> Both arms and hands were so dreadfully shattered as to render necessary the removal of the left arm high up under the shoulder and the right below the elbow. This was skilfully affected by Mr. Bond and his sufferings were born with extraordinary fortitude and hopes remain of his recovery; a subscription has been opened to aid in his support.

Food and Drink

Rose & Crown (Eli's), Huish Episcopi, 01458 250494 – Although just over a mile from Muchelney this seventeenth-century thatched inn known locally as Eli's has been in the same family for generations and is worth a visit. It still retains its unusual features and original character, after being severely flooded three years ago. A rare counter-less flagstoned taproom adjoins several cosy rooms. Somerset CAMRA pub of the season 2014.

White Hart Inn, Market Place, Somerton – The White Hart has been trading as an inn in Somerton's market square since the sixteenth century. There are eight en-suite letting rooms and the inn was named as one of the best affordable places to stay by the *Sunday Times* in 2017. The inn is much larger inside than you might first envisage and there are plenty of tables for breakfast, lunch and dinner as well as coffee and cakes – www.whitehartsomerton.com.

Halfway House, Pitney Hill, Pitney, Langport.TA10 9AB. 01458 272273 – An outstanding pub serving eight to nine regional ales on hand pump alongside many bottled beers and real ciders. The inside is very traditional with flagstone flooring, old solid wooden tables and benches and three real fires. This busy pub has been in the *Good Beer Guide* for twenty-five years and gained the ultimate award of National Pub of the Year in 1996. Superb homecooked food including a roast lunch served on Sundays – www.thehalfwayhouse.co.uk.

The Muddled Man Inn, Lower Street, West Chinnock, TA18 7PT. 01935 881 235 – Family run free house, serving a range of West Country ales from three handpumps, plus guest beers straight from the cask. Good food available, the Sunday lunch is popular and needs to be booked. Burrowhill cider is also available. The pub is fully wheelchair-accessible with a disabled toilet situated within the entrance hall and slopes on the ground floor to all public areas – www.themuddledmaninn.co.uk.

The Brewers Arms 18 St James Street, South Petherton,TA13 5BW. 01460 241887 – A mile from the A303. Dating from the seventeenth century, this old coaching inn has much to offer with its lively village bar, an extensive range of ales, relaxed dining rooms and three en-suite bedrooms. The Brewers Arms has been awarded 'Taste of the West' silver and gold awards, Western Gazette Pub of the Year in 2013 and was Somerset CAMRA Pub of the Year for the third time in 2016 – www.the-brewersarms.com.

CHAPTER 5

Mendip District

This section sees several towns and cities which in a general tourist guidebook would warrant a chapter to themselves: Street, Glastonbury, Wells, Shepton Mallet and Frome, to name just a few. As it is, they are also of highly historical importance and this is, of course, what we shall be focusing on. We left the previous section in the Bruton area, so it is

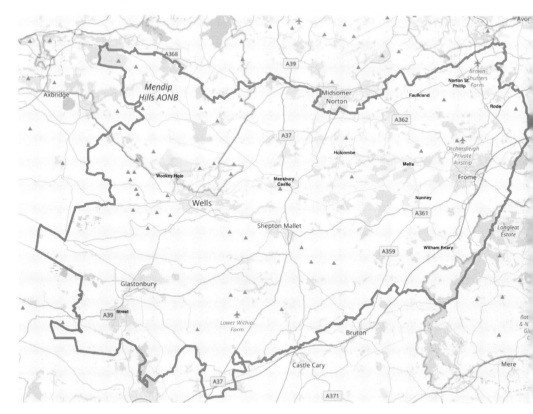

Map of Mendip District.

suggested we travel up the A359, with the town behind us and head towards our first stop in this latest area: **Nunney** (www.nunney.org).

Located within the village and well worth a visit are the imposing ruins of **Nunney Castle** (www.english-heritage.org.uk/visit/places/nunney-castle). The castle was built by John de la Mare in 1373 with the proceeds of his adventure during the 100 Years War. Its use was as much domestic as military, and it passed into the hands of the Prater family in around 1578. The family supported the Royalist cause during the Civil War and, not surprisingly, Nunney was besieged by Cromwell's men under Lord Fairfax. After a short siege, during which its walls were heavily pounded by cannon, Prater surrendered and the building fell into disrepair. On Christmas Day 1910 the north wall collapsed and much of the stone carted away for reuse. Nunney Castle is now under the care of English Heritage and entrance is free.

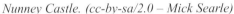

Nunney Castle. (cc-by-sa/2.0 – Mick Searle)

Just down the road is **Frome** (www.discoverfrome.co.uk). In recent years this market town has repeatedly made national headlines as one of the most pleasant and popular places to live, but this belies a rich historical heritage and a dark and bloody past. At well over 300, it has more listed buildings than any other town in Somerset and was for a long time, until around the middle of the seventeenth century, bigger than Bath. It made its reputation initially as a cloth and textile centre and was renowned for its blue cloth.

Frome Museum (www.fromemuseum.wordpress.com) stands at 1 North Parade, its Italianate building was built as a Literary and Scientific Institute in 1865 and is Grade II listed. Among its many collections is an important assemblage of artefacts from the bronze foundry of J.W. Singer, which boasts among its most famous castings around the world: 'Boudica & Her Daughters' on the Embankment, 'Lady Justice' atop the Old Bailey and 'King Alfred' at Winchester. A display is also devoted to the former Butler and Tanner printing works in the town, including an old printing press. Other display exhibits include plans, photographs, diagrams and tools from James Fussell's Ironworks of nearby Mells, and a street that has a row of shops such as a blacksmith, chemist shop and a pub; along with a collection of Victorian and later costumes.

There is limited evidence of Roman settlement in the town, but the remains of a villa at **Whatley** (www.visitnunney.com/roman-villa-whatley-combe) and the discover of the Frome Hoard in nearby **Witham Friary** show the Romans were certainly nearby. According to author Annette Burkitt in her book, *Flesh and Bones: of Frome Selwood and Wessex*, Frome was a favourite place to visit by certain kings in Saxon times, including Athelstan, the grandson of Alfred The Great. At a Christmas Witan in AD 934, a charter was signed which laid the foundation of England as the unified state we know it today.

The **Duke of Monmouth** stayed in Frome during his rebellion, in 1685. His three-day sojourn in the town wasn't very productive, as during this time he received news of the Earl of Argyll's defeat in Scotland (Argyll's Rising, as it was called, had been timed to coincide with Monmouth's own revolt). With that in mind, Monmouth called a war council and was all for calling it a day and returning to the Continent. In the end, he was persuaded to continue, and so sealed his fate at Sedgemoor.

General Montgomery used the **Portway Hotel**, in Frome, during the Second World War, as his headquarters in the aftermath of Dunkirk.

The plan was that his Third Division would regroup in the town and surrounding areas, be re-equipped and then set off back across the Channel. Before this could happen, however, France fell, and Montgomery and his Division were sent to the south coast for home defence. The Portway is now private flats named Montgomery Court and a plaque on its outer wall commemorates the famous soldier's brief stay in the town during June 1940.

In 1851, Frome was also the scene of an infamous Victorian murder. A colleague of Inspector Whicher (see Constance Kent below), Detective Sergeant Henry Smith, duly came down from London to investigate the brutal rape and murder of 14-year-old Sarah Watts. Together with the savage killing of Francis Saville Kent in Rode nine years later, this was probably one of the most sickening and repulsive crimes in Victorian Somerset. The full

The Lamb & Fountain.

account was told for the first time in *The Awful Killing of Sarah Watts* by the authors of this current volume.

Near to Frome is the village of Rode. Here is the **Devil's Bed and Bolster**; a collection of large stones, and all that remains of a chambered long-barrow on a hill to the south-east of Rode. They are shaded by large horse chestnut trees, at the edge of a field on a 'conservation walk' permissive path. It was in Rode that one of the most infamous murders of the Victorian Age took place (see below). It was a quirk of geographical and administrative division that the house in which the murder took place fell within the county of Wiltshire, while the village itself belonged to Somerset.

Also, in Rode is **St Lawrence Church.** The illustration below is from 1848 and is by local artist William Walter Wheatley; the original is in the West of England Art Gallery in Bristol, and a copy hangs in the church.

Wheatley's painting of Rode Church in 1848.

It depicts a ceremony known as 'clipping the church', an ancient custom traditionally held on Easter Monday or Shrove Tuesday. Little is known about the history of the custom; the earliest known written records date from the late fourteenth and early fifteenth centuries, but the word 'clipping' is probably Anglo-Saxon in origin and derived from the word 'clyppan', meaning 'embrace' or 'clasp'. The event involves the church congregation or local children holding hands in an outward-facing ring around the building. When the circle is completed, onlookers will cheer shout and sing. The custom is repeated here every two years.

The Road Hill Murder of 1860

During the night of 29 June 1860, a 3-year-old boy disappeared from his bed at a large country house in the village of Road in North Somerset, five miles from Frome. The child was Francis Saville Kent, the son of a factory inspector and his second wife Mary Ann. The house was secure apart from a slightly open window and there were no signs of a forced entry. After an intensive search involving people from the village, his body was found in the vault of a privy with extensive knife wounds and his throat cut.

The local constables were baffled by the crime and a Detective Inspector Jack Whicher was called in from Scotland Yard. He reached the conclusion that the murder was committed by a member of the household and suspicion fell on the little boy's half-sister Constance, who was questioned but released. Understandably there was much rumour and speculation – the father Samuel Kent was known to be unfaithful as a husband and had been having an affair with a servant girl (now his second wife) while his first wife lay dying. Nothing could be proven, and the crime seemed destined to remain unsolved.

By 1865 the family had moved away, and Constance was at a French finishing school. In that year, totally unexpectedly, she confessed her guilt to a clergyman Arthur Wagner and told him of her determination to give herself up. Constance appeared before the magistrates and confessed that she had waited until the family and servants were asleep before taking the child into the privy and cutting his throat with her father's razor. She offered no motive for the deed, but it is widely assumed that it was an act of spite and revenge against her father and stepmother, whom she thought loved little Francis more than her and her brother William; both were children of his first marriage.

Her confession and trial called intense interest which continues to this day. She pleaded guilty and was sentenced to death, but this was later commuted to life imprisonment due to her age at the time of the crime and her confession.

Her conviction did not stop the rumours, and some believe to this day that the crime was either committed by her father, or that she committed it in conjunction with her young brother William. Constance served a total of twenty years in jail and was released in 1885 at the age of 41, after which she emigrated to Australia and worked as a nurse under an assumed name before dying at the age of 100 in 1944.

The church itself is thought to be late fourteenth century and was 'restored' in 1874 by Charles Edward Davis. St Lawrence is a Grade I listed building and it is likely that there was a previous church on the same site, as some fragments of a Norman doorway survive. Local legend has it that King Charles II surveyed the countryside from the top of the tower, after the Battle of Worcester on 3 September 1651, to see if any pursuing Parliamentary troops were in the vicinity. The church underwent significant work to the gallery and bells in 1774. The tower has contained bells since the sixteenth century, and in 1753 Thomas Bilbie of Chew Stoke cast a new peel of six bells, one was recast by the Whitechapel Bell Foundry in 1817. These hung in the tower into the twentieth century but were not used because of concerns about the strength of the wooden frame. This was replaced by one made of steel between 2003 and 2006 when the bells were rededicated and rang out once more.

The name of the village was spelt 'Road' until 1919 when it was changed to Rode, presumably it was thought that the former would have been confusing. According to legend the original village, or part of it, lay on the same side of the A361 as the church, but was destroyed by fire, possibly in medieval times, and some odd lumps and bumps can be seen in the adjoining field and are definitely worth investigating.

The range of buildings opposite the Cross Keys pub was once one building, possibly the market hall, while the roof timbers are original throughout and have been dated to 1428.

On leaving Rode, head north and soon the village of **Norton St Philip** is reached. After Sedgemoor this is probably one of, if not the most important locations during the brief Monmouth Rebellion. Only fourteen minutes from Bath, and dissected by the B3110, unfortunately this village of great charm and history is blighted by the lorries and heavy traffic that thunder through its heart daily. Nevertheless, it is the location of the **George Inn** (www. georgeinnnsp.co.uk) which is one of several pubs that claim to be Britain's oldest tavern and dates from at least 1327 and is arguably one of the most famous pubs in the country. It started life as a wool store for the priory at Hinton Charterhouse and was big enough to accommodate travellers and merchants coming to the annual wool fairs that were held in the village from the late thirteenth century until 1902. In the fifteenth century the timber-framed upper floors were added, and the inn soon became part of

The George Inn, Norton St Phillip. © Maigheach-gheal (cc-by-sa/2.0)

the stagecoach route between London and the South West. The beamed bar features a distinctive fireplace. There are several other rooms used for drinking and dining, including a large dining room at the rear and a dungeon bar, both accessed from the attractive cobbled courtyard. Steps lead from the car park to an enclosed garden which has views across the mead to the church. On 12 June 1668 the diarist **Samuel Pepys** passed through Norton St Philip with his wife and servants on their way to Bath from Salisbury. It is a favourite setting for films and television dramas.

The George Inn & The Monmouth Rebellion

The village of Norton St Phillip was the site of a battle during the Monmouth Rebellion of 1685 and the inn was used as its headquarters by the rebel army after their march from Keynsham via the southern outskirts of Bath. Monmouth arrived at the village with his followers late in the evening of 26 June 1685, and made the George Inn his headquarters, with billets being sought for his men, and stables for the horses, throughout the village. They hauled four guns up the steep inclines of the village and Norton become an armed camp.

One story is that while Monmouth sat at a table in a room on the first floor of the inn, a shot rang out, the bullet shattering the window and just missing the duke who had a price of £1,000, dead or alive, on his head. The circular mahogany dining-table at which he sat, with an inscribed brass plate, was on view in the same room until the 1970s.

Having avoided the assassin's bullet, Monmouth was preparing to move southwards on the 27th, when news came of the approaching advance guard of the Royal Army. He was a talented soldier and believing himself to be in a sound defensive position, he decided to stand and fight. Monmouth set up a strong barricade in North Street, which in those days was the main road out of the village towards Bath. This is where the main fighting took place, with the king's troops trying to break the barricade, and blood flowing down the lane. The turning point came when Monmouth led a flank attack, infiltrating troops through the grounds of a large house which then stood immediately to the east of the road. There was some drawn-out artillery action, in heavy rain, which lasted for six hours before the king's army withdrew to Bradford-on-Avon. The skirmish had cost them eighty dead. The rebels lost only eighteen men – a tribute to Monmouth's leadership. Cannonballs have been ploughed up in the fields to the north of the village.

After Monmouth's defeat at Sedgemoor, treatment of the captured rebels was swift and bloody. The George was used as a court by Judge Jefferies and twelve executions carried out on the village common, known as Churchmead or The Mead, as part of the Bloody Assizes. One story goes that as the condemned men were led to their execution behind the Fleur De Lys pub a village lad who helpfully held the gate open got swept along with them and was strung up as well despite his protests!

The church of **SS Phillip and James** dates in part from the thirteenth century and contains the grave, or at least a memorial to **'The Fair Maids of Foscott'**. The Maids were Siamese twins first mentioned by diarist Samuel Pepys in June of 1668 when he visited the church and saw their tomb.

At Philips Norton I walked to the church, and there saw a very ancient tomb of some Knight Templar, I think; and here saw the tombstone whereon there were only two heads cut, which, the story goes, and credibly, were two sisters called the Fair Maids of Foscott, that had two bodies upward and one belly and there lie buried. Here is also a very fine ring of six bells, and they mighty tuneable.

(www.pepysdiary.com/diary/1668/06/12/)

Tradition has it that they lived to reach a 'state of maturity and that one of them dying the survivor was constrained to drag about her lifeless companion until death released her of her horrid burden'. Given the twins must have been one of the wonders of the age it is strange that so little is known about them, including their names and even the century in which they lived. When Pepys saw the tomb, the effigy of the two sisters was cut in stone on the floor of the nave. This was removed probably as part of a restoration in the 1840s, except for the two heads which were saved and fixed to the wall inside the tower. Foscott is a hamlet, a few miles from Norton, now named Foxcote.

The Fair Maids of Foscott.

Near Norton St Philip is **Farleigh Hungerford Castle** (www.english-heritage.org.uk/visit/places/farleigh-hungerford-castle), which was constructed between 1377 and 1383 by Sir Thomas Hungerford, who made his fortune as steward to John of Gaunt. The castle was built on the site of an existing manor house overlooking the River Frome and when a deer park was attached to the castle it required the destruction of an entire village. Sir Thomas's son, Sir Walter Hungerford, a leading courtier to Henry V, became rich during the Hundred Years War with France and extended the castle enclosing the parish church in the process. By his death in 1449, the castle was richly appointed, and its chapel decorated with murals. It remained in the hands of the Hungerford family over the next two centuries, apart from periods during the War of the Roses in which it was briefly held by the Crown, following the execution of many of the family. By the outbreak of the civil war in 1642 the castle had been modernised to the latest Tudor and Stuart fashions and was held by Sir Edward Hungerford who declared his support for Parliament, and became a leader of the Roundheads in Wiltshire. Farleigh Hungerford was seized by Royalist forces in 1643 but recaptured by Parliament without a fight near the end of the conflict in 1645 and managed to escape the demolition that was the fate of many other castles in the south-west of England.

The stocks and standing stones on Faulkland Green in 1907.

The last member of the family to hold the castle, Sir Edward Hungerford, inherited it in 1657, but his gambling and extravagance forced him to sell up in 1686. By the eighteenth century the castle was no longer occupied and fell into disrepair. In 1915, it was sold to the Office of Works and a controversial restoration programme began. It is now a tourist attraction operated by English Heritage.

Heading west, back towards the heart of the county, we come to the picturesque village of **Faulkland**. On its green and at several other sites throughout the village, there are standing stones of unknown origin. Between two of the stones are the sixteenth- or seventeenth-century village stocks.

A public house with an ancient and protected interior is **Tuckers Grave Inn,** (www.tuckersgraveinn.co.uk) just outside Faulkland and about a mile down the A366. The building dates from the early eighteenth century and it is one of Somerset's most famous inns and is Grade II listed. Its unusual name is derived from the suicide of local farm worker Edward Tucker, who hanged himself from a beam at nearby Charlton farm in 1747 and was buried at the crossroads. This event was featured in the song 'Tucker's Grave' by 1970s punk band The Stranglers, who are regulars there. Built in the mid-seventeenth century as a farmhouse, it became an inn in 1827 and has an interior of national importance; it is one of the few remaining pubs with no bar counter, selling traditional cider and real ale from an alcove. Shove-ha'penny is played and there is a skittle alley.

South from Faulkland is the village of **Mells** (www.mellsvillage.co.uk). The grave of war poet Siegfried Sassoon can be found in the churchyard of **St Andrews,** along with a stone, no longer legible, which once read:

All my inward friends abhorred me and they whom I loved have turned against me. My kinsfolk have failed me and my familiar friends have forgotten me. William Leecox husband of Rachel Leecox departed April ye sixteenth 1700.

He must have been greatly missed.... The church is to be found in New Street and although it is recorded as belonging to Glastonbury Abbey in 1292, it dates predominantly from the late fifteenth century, built in the Perpendicular style with the inevitable mid-nineteenth century restoration.

The tower erected in 1446 has a clock from the seventeenth century with a ring of eight bells hung for change ringing, the earliest of which dates from 1716. That bell, the fourth of the ring, and the seventh, cast a year later, were made by the first Abraham Rudhall of the bellfounders, Rudhall of Gloucester. Two more (the third and eighth) were cast in 1745 by Thomas Bilbie, and the sixth (1788) by William Bilbie, both the latter of the renowned Bilbie family of bellfounders. The other three bells, (the first, second and fifth) were cast in 1869 by Mears & Stainbank of the Whitechapel Bell Foundry. There is also a sanctus bell, hung in the roof of the chancel, which dates from around 1325 and is on the national database of historically important bells. As well as being the location of Siegfried Sassoon's grave, Sir Maurice Bonham-Carter, the Liberal peer and cricketer, is buried there.

During the nineteenth and early twentieth centuries, Mells and surrounding villages had several coal mines, much of which would have supplied the ironworks of James Fussell. The Old Ironstone Works is a biological Site of Special Scientific Interest due to its population of Greater and Lesser Horseshoe bats. The site is now a ruin but at one time it produced agricultural edge-tools that were exported all over the world, and now has a unique and major importance in relation to industrial archaeology. The block of buildings adjacent to the entrance is listed Grade II and most of the rest of the site is a Scheduled Ancient Monument.

Mells Manor (www.mellsvillage.co.uk/mells-manor) was the home to the Horner family, who had a close association with the Asquiths, renowned for their influence on British political and intellectual life. Charles I stayed there in July 1644, even though Sir John Horner was a Parliamentarian who was later to be taken prisoner at Bristol, resisting Prince Rupert. His son, Sir George, was a Royalist, and his great-grandson Colonel Thomas Strangways Horner MP (1688–1742) was even suspected of Jacobite sympathies. In 1716, after the first rebellion, they came to arrest him at the manor, but he slipped out of the house and walked away, disguised as a drover, to Smithfield in London, finally emerging in the House of Commons to clear his name. The house is not open to the public. The **War Memorial** was designed by Sir Edward Lutyens, designer of the cenotaph in London and there is an annual fair and **Daffodil Festival** (www.mellsdaffodilfestival.co.uk) which is held on Easter Monday.

Heading west from Mells is **Holcombe** (www.holcombevillage.weebly.com). A mile from the village, down a farm track and through fields, is the **Church of S. Andrew.** The church has late Saxon and early Norman origins, but was largely rebuilt in the sixteenth century. It is now redundant and has been in the care of the Churches Conservation Trust since 1987. The church has a two-stage tower and two-bay nave and the interior includes late-Georgian box pews and a Jacobean pulpit. In the graveyard is a memorial to the family of Robert Falcon Scott, whose father managed the brewery in the village. There is also a yew tree thought to be about 1,500 years old. The church is still used for weddings and was one of the locations for the more recent version of the television series Poldark. Access is via the Churches Conservation Trust and the key is kept locally.

Further west is **Maesbury Castle**, within the parish of Croscombe on the Mendip Hills. This is an Iron Age hill fort, to the north of Shepton Mallet. The name is derived from 'maes', meaning 'field' or 'plain' in Brythonic Welsh, and 'burh', meaning 'fort' in Old English. There is also a record of the name 'Merksburi' in AD 705, meaning 'boundary fort'. The area was a boundary between the Romano-British Celts and West Saxons during the period 577-652, when the nearby Wansdyke fortification was part of the border. The enclosure has an area of two acres and lies at a height of 950ft with great views in many directions including the Somerset Levels, Glastonbury Tor and Brent Knoll, which are the closest and probably the most easily identifiable landmarks from the site. The fort has a single rampart up to 19ft high, with an outer ditch (univallate) with entrances to the south-east and north-east. The site and surrounding grounds are now owned by the Stevens family, who have been farming in Somerset for over sixty years.

To the south of Maesbury Castle lays the town of **Shepton Mallet** (www.visitsheptonmallet.co.uk). The route of the **Fosse Way,** the main Roman road into south-west England, runs through it and there is evidence of a settlement from that period. It also contains a medieval parish church and many other listed buildings. It was an important wool centre in medieval times, but this was later replaced in the eighteenth century by industries such as brewing. Shepton Mallet remains a prominent producer of cider and close by is the Royal Bath and West of England Society's showground. During the Civil War, the town supported the Parliamentary side, but a bloodless confrontation in August 1642 between the king's supporters and those of Parliament seems to be the extent of its involvement. A while later, the Monmouth Rebellion saw the Duke of Monmouth pass through Shepton Mallet, staying at Longbridge House in Cowl Street, on his way to capture Bristol. He failed and a week later he was back – on his way to Sedgemoor. After his defeat there, he headed in this direction once more spending a night at Downside, a mile north of the town.

The prison at **Shepton Mallet** (www.sheptonmalletprison.com) was built in 1610, following an Act introduced by King James I which stated that all counties had to have their own 'House of Correction'; Shepton Mallet was the oldest working prison in the United Kingdom up until its closure at the end of March 2013. The original land was purchased from Reverend Edward Barnards for a cost of £160 and when built, the prison could hold men, women and children together. Debtors, thieves, misfits, vagrants and the mentally ill were sentenced to long periods. Although it was pretty common in prisons of the time for favours by jailors to result in promiscuous behaviour, lax discipline and primitive sanitation led to regular outbreaks of gaol fever, ulcers, jaundice, asthma, itch and venereal diseases. The only real medical aid was the local doctor being called in to pronounce a death, following which bodies were taken to an unconsecrated burial ground, just outside the prison. The door in the wall on Frithfield Lane still exists, as do nine unmarked graves within the grounds. It was common practice with British executions to bury prisoners in this way. The prison has a long history of execution by both hanging and firing squad; the hanging room still exists, but has been used as office space for many years. Following the Monmouth Rebellion of 1685 at least twelve Shepton men were executed for having sympathised with the rebels; their bowels were burned and their heads placed on poles around the town.

The prison closed in 1930 due to lack of use, as by then it held an average of just fifty-one prisoners. It reopened in 1939 as a British military prison and soon housed 300 men from all the armed services, some being placed in huts in the prison yard. Between 1942 and 1945 it was run as an American military prison, housing 768 soldiers; by the end of 1944, it was guarded by twelve officers and eighty-two enlisted men. During this period eighteen American servicemen were executed, sixteen hanged and two shot by firing squad. During the war the prison also housed the Domesday book, Magna Carta, HMS *Victory* logbooks and many other historical documents kept safe from the German bombing raids. At one point over 300 documents were housed there, occupying the former women's wing. Some had to be moved again (not the Domesday book) when Bristol and Bath began suffering German air-raids; the documents were spread to different locations to reduce the risk of the entire collection being destroyed.

The jail returned to British military use in September 1945 and was used primarily for servicemen due to be discharged after serving their sentence. Soldiers held there included the Kray twins, who were serving out their National Service after absconding, and it was here that they met Charlie Richardson. The last military death sentence at the jail was carried out in 1945, while the last civilian to be hanged there was John Lincoln in 1926, for fatally shooting 25-year-old Edward Richards in Trowbridge on Christmas Eve the previous year. The list of executioners employed by the jail included Thomas and Albert Pierrepoint before the return of the prison to civilian use in 1966; the gallows were removed in 1967.

The first escape on record was in 1765, and the last in 1993, when three prisoners descended the prison wall using the traditional 'knotted sheets' method, after tunnelling through a 2ft wall; they were soon recaptured. The jail has some of the highest prison walls in the country at 75ft.

West Shepton, which forms the south-west corner of the town, is dominated by the Grade II listed building that was the former **Shepton Mallet Union Workhouse** (www.workhouses.org.uk/SheptonMallet). It was originally constructed in 1848 and later became the Norah Fry Mental Hospital. It has now been converted into flats but is still worth seeing.

To the east of the town is the site of the **Cranmore East Somerset Railway** (www.eastsomersetrailway.com) which is a heritage railway line and museum, located at the old station. It contains a red telephone box that incorporates a stamp machine and post box produced around 1927 – one of only fifty made. Opposite the platform, there is a signal box dating from 1904, which is in the standard Great Western Railway pattern of the period. These days the line runs between Cranmore and Mendip Vale, but prior to the Beeching axe, the railway was part of the Cheddar

Valley line that ran from Witham to Yatton, meeting the Somerset and Dorset Joint Railway at Wells. Heading west again, we arrive at what is the smallest city in England. **Wells** (www.wellssomerset.com) has a population of around 10,500, who are dominated by one thing: **Wells Cathedral** (www.wellscathedral.org.uk). It was built between 1175 and 1490 and the current building is a significant landmark in Somerset and the South West. As well as its iconic West Front, which contains one of the largest galleries of medieval sculpture in the world, it has unique features that separate it from other English cathedrals, including the beautiful 'scissor arches' supporting the central tower; a structure which was added in 1338 after the weight of a new spire on the top of the tower threatened to collapse the whole building. It has one of the largest collections of historic stained glass in the country, including the Jesse Window, one of the most splendid examples of fourteenth century stained glass in Europe, which narrowly escaped destruction during the civil war. Among its treasures the cathedral boasts the famous Wells Clock which is said to be the second oldest clock mechanism in the country; the fascinating octagonal Chapter House; and one of only four chained libraries in the UK. Entry is free but donations are 'enthusiastically encouraged'.

Another fascinating place to visit within the vicinity is the **Bishops Palace**, (www.bishopspalace.org.uk) a splendid medieval palace that has been the home of the Bishops of Bath & Wells for more than 800 years. The building was begun around 1210 by Bishop Jocelin of Wells, but dates in the main from 1230, with the chapel built between 1275 and 1292 for Bishop Robert Burnell. The gatehouse has a bridge over the moat, and dates from 1341. The first bishop received a crown licence to build a residence and deer park to the south of the cathedral. The palace was restored and had an upper storey added by Benjamin Ferrey between 1846 and 1854. Within the fortified palace walls lie the ruin of the Great Hall, the Bishop's private chapel, and 14 acres of gardens, including an arboretum, Community Garden and Garden of Reflection. This uniquely moated palace has an imposing gatehouse with portcullis and drawbridge, which give the impression that you may be entering a castle structure, but inside is a peaceful and tranquil residence for the visitor to enjoy.

The **Wells & Mendip Museum** (www.wellsmuseum.org.uk), sited at 8 Cathedral Green, was founded in 1893 by Herbert Balch. Balch was a naturalist, caver and geologist who pioneered many techniques used by modern cavers. His fine collection of local artefacts and memorabilia form the core of the museum's displays, which retains the best qualities of a private Victorian museum and comprises examples of geology and fossils collected from the Mendip Hills, many of which date from prehistoric times. Other exhibits include lead ingots from Roman Britain and statuary from Wells Cathedral. The collection is housed in the former Chancellors' House, which has fifteenth-century origins, although most of the current fabric of the building is from the seventeenth and eighteenth centuries.

Meanwhile, **Vicars' Close** is claimed to be the oldest purely residential street with original buildings surviving intact in Europe. The historian John Julius Norwich calls it 'that rarest of survivals, a planned street of the mid-fourteenth century'. It contains numerous Grade I listed buildings, and consists of twenty-seven residences (originally forty-four) built for Bishop Ralph of Shrewsbury, a chapel and library at the north end, and a hall at the south end, over an arched gate. It is connected at its southern end to the cathedral by way of a walkway over Chain Gate. Also of interest is the **City Arms** in Wells High Street which was once the main town prison.

To the north-west of Wells is **Wookey Hole Cave** (www.wookey.co.uk). These are a series of limestone caverns, with a show cave and tourist attractions in the village of Wookey, sat on the southern edge of the Mendip Hills near Wells. The River Axe flows through the cave and is a Site of Special Scientific Interest for biological and geological reasons. Wookey Hole cave is what is known as a 'solutional cave', one that is formed by a process of weathering in which the natural acid in groundwater dissolves the rocks. Some of the water originates as the rain that flows into streams on impervious rocks on the plateau before sinking at the limestone boundary into cave systems such as Swildon's Hole, Eastwater Cavern and St Cuthbert's Swallet; the rest of the rain percolates directly through the limestone. The temperature in the caves is a constant 11°C, which means that they are ideal for maturing Cheddar cheese. The discovery of tools and fossilised animal remains from the Palaeolithic period show the caves have been in use by humans for around 45,000 years. There is evidence of

Stone and Iron Age occupation which continued into the Roman period. A corn-grinding mill operated on the resurgent waters of the River Axe as early as the Domesday survey of 1086 and the waters of the river are used in a handmade-paper mill, which began operations in about 1610, making it the oldest in Britain.

Seemingly inextricably linked and as historically important is **Glastonbury** (www.visitsomerset.co.uk/explore-somerset/glastonbury). Like its close neighbour it is dominated by its religious buildings, although it does have the added attraction of its famous tor. Although its population is greater than Wells, it is a town, not a city, and most famous for its ancient Abbey (www.glastonburyabbey.com), which was founded in the seventh century but was largely destroyed by a major fire in 1184. In desperate need of funds for rebuilding, the monks announced they had discovered the grave and bones of St Patrick. This failed to convince many prospective pilgrims, so another discovery was made – the bones of St Dunstan, a popular saint who had at least some connection to the site having been abbot there in AD 946. Unfortunately, it seems that he was also buried in Canterbury and again the pilgrims were unimpressed.

Six years later the monks made yet another incredible discovery – the bones of the legendary King Arthur and his Queen Guinevere – and this time everything fell into place. Glastonbury could be equated with Avalon, the fabled resting place of the dead king. The skeletons were supposedly found in a hollowed oak tree buried between two pyramids, that of Arthur was of gigantic size befitting a great hero king, and so that there could be no dispute this time they also found a lead plaque bearing Arthur's name. In fairness to the monks of old, when the site was excavated by professional archaeologist Raleigh Radford in 1962, he found a great pit had indeed been dug where the monks claimed – though what they found there is anyone's guess. The finds fired the popular imagination and the paying public flocked in – and still do so today. The abbey was rebuilt and by the fourteenth century it had become one of the richest and most powerful monasteries in the country, controlling large areas of land and resources.

During the dissolution of the monasteries in 1539 the abbot, Richard Whiting, refused to surrender the abbey and was accused of treason. Found guilty, and despite his great age, he was dragged to the top of Glastonbury

Glastonbury Tor. It can get windy!

Tor and hanged, drawn and quartered. The abbey was by now deserted, but even so his head was set up over the west gate and his limbs displayed at Wells, Bath, Ilchester and Bridgwater. The abbey was stripped of everything of value and fell into disrepair, surviving as the ruin we see today.

Meanwhile, **Glastonbury Tor** (www.nationaltrust.org.uk/glastonbury-tor) dominates the landscape for miles. This imposing hill is topped by the roofless St Michael's Tower, a Grade I listed building managed by the National Trust. Given its stunning appearance, amid the flat Somerset plains, it is not surprising that the tower has attracted attention from the earliest times with indications of occupation as far back as the Iron Age. The present tower was constructed in the fourteenth century, replacing a wooden structure that was destroyed by an earthquake in 1275, and has been restored several times since. Access is free and all year round, and the view is breathtaking; it is a very steep slope though and care should be taken in wet or windy weather.

Glastonbury Lake Village Museum can be found at 9 High Street and occupies a fifteenth-century merchant's house, which contains Iron Age possessions and works of art from the site, preserved in almost perfect condition in the peat after the village was abandoned. The village itself is one of the country's best-preserved examples of a prehistoric crannog or man-made island, which was discovered in 1892 and excavated over the next fifteen years. Of a similar age and nature to the lake village, and only five miles distant at Shapwick, is an ancient wood trackway named **The Sweet Track** after its finder, Ray Sweet. Its construction has been dated to 3807 BC, putting it firmly in the Neolithic period. It ran for 1.2 miles, across marshy ground between Shapwick and what was at the time an island at Westhay and was part of a network that crossed the Somerset Levels. The track was very narrow, consisting of crossed wooden poles in an 'X' formation hammered into the ground with oak planks laid end to end in the upper part of the X section. Most of the timbers have been left in place and are carefully monitored so that they don't dry out and disintegrate.

Also, in the High Street, is the **George & Pilgrims Hotel,** which was built in the late fifteenth century to accommodate visitors to Glastonbury Abbey and is a Grade I listed building; this is one of the oldest purpose-built public houses in the South West. Originally the Pilgrims'

Inn of Glastonbury Abbey, but by the mid-nineteenth century the building was known as the George Hotel. Hence the current name. The front of the three-storey building is divided into three tiers of panels with traceried heads. Above these are three carved panels bearing the coats of arms of the abbey and of King Edward IV.

Another local attraction in Glastonbury is the **Somerset Rural Life Museum**, (www.swheritage.org.uk/somerset-rural-life-museum) situated at Abbey Farm in Chilkwell Street, which is a collection of the county's social and agricultural history, housed in buildings surrounding a fourteenth-century barn that once belonged to the abbey. Meanwhile, the **Abbot's Fish House** in Meare, three miles north-west of Glastonbury, was built in the fourteenth century and is the only surviving monastic fishery building in England. Fishing was an important source of food for the monks of Glastonbury Abbey and carried out in artificial ponds, which were mentioned at Meare in the Domesday Book. The present rectangular stone building was constructed by the abbot between 1322 and 1335 for the storage and processing of the fish and as a residence for the chief fisherman. After the dissolution of the monasteries the building fell into disrepair and was seriously damaged by fire in the 1880s. Some restoration has been undertaken during the twentieth century, including the replacement of the roof in the 1920s.

Clark's Shoe Museum (www.the-shoe-museum.org) in Street, houses more than 1,500 shoes from Roman to modern day and tells the story of Clarks from its beginnings in the early nineteenth century. There are four galleries which showcase the development of the footwear industry in Street and items on display include shoemaking machinery and tools, advertising materials and hundreds of shoes. The earliest shoe on display is a second-century girls' sandal sole and there are Roman shoes, which were found locally near Langport. Medieval shoes from London are also on show, along with a beautiful collection of Georgian and Victorian shoes made from a wide range of materials such as satin, silk brocade, linen, wool and kid leather. There are also buckles and Edwardian side-button boots and high-lace boots. A selection of footwear from around the world includes an Emir's slipper from Nigeria, a Chinese shoe for a bound foot, kub kobs worn in Turkish baths, and Finnish shoes made from birch bark.

Clarks shoes include a Brown Petersburg, which was the first shoe made by Clarks, shoes from 1885, and the earliest women's shoe from 1856. Items from the extensive Clarks archives are also on display and visitors can see the original 1828 indenture of James Clark who, with his elder brother Cyrus, founded the footwear business. Highlights of the museum include Princess Diana's wedding slipper, a replica of the shoes worn by the queen when she married Prince Philip, and a 1923 Perugia ladies' gold, black and silver bar shoe.

Food and Drink

Old Bath Arms, 1 Palmer Street, Frome, BA11 1DS. 01373 465045 – The maze-like layout of this town centre pub consists of a lively public bar, a quiet lounge, a, restaurant with a beer garden and smoking area to the rear. The excellent food menu comprises traditional pub food, steaks, tapas and paella as well as Sunday roasts. There are also pizzas cooked in the pub's own wood-fired pizza oven. It is one of the few pubs to sell real cider and has a changing list of suppliers which include Thatcher's Cheddar Valley. Live music includes a pub pianist (with the piano intriguingly situated on a raised area overlooking Findlay's Real Ale Bar) and a traditional violinist. There are murals and paintings by local artists on display throughout the pub. Bed and Breakfast available.

Lamb & Fountain, 57 Castle Street, Frome, BA11 3BW. 01373 463414 – A Grade II listed building and on the CAMRA register as 'An historic pub interior of regional importance' having been untouched since the 1960s. A small and very friendly pub with fantastic views over the town. Hidden under a trapdoor is an ancient ice house which is surrounded by a maze of cellars and tunnels. Landlady Freda Searle has the honour of being one of the country's oldest landladies aged 97 in 2019, having run the pub for 50 years. 'Mothers', as it is affectionally known is situated in the Trinity area of the town which is an area of national significance as an example of early industrial housing. The place is a gem, and cider is the main tipple of the locals.

The Blue Boar, 15 Market Place, Frome, BA11 1AN. 01373 302 851 – Dating from 1691 this unpretentious family-run pub in the centre of town serves one real ale, which changes regularly, a selection of real cider, homecooked food and old-world charm. Rooms are also available – www.discoverfrome.co.uk/attraction/the-blue-boar.

Tuckers Grave Inn, Faulkland, BA3 5XF. 01373 834 230 – About a mile down the A366 lies the historic Tuckers Grave Inn dating from the early eighteenth century. Its unusual name is derived from the suicide of local farm worker Edward Tucker who hanged himself from a beam at nearby Charlton farm in 1747 and was buried at the crossroads and featured in a song by 1970s' punk band The Stranglers who are regulars there. A gem from a bygone age and with a nationally important historic pub interior, this place was built in the mid-seventeenth century as a farmhouse, became an inn in 1827, and has changed little since. There is no bar, and the beers and ciders are served from an alcove. Shove-ha'penny is played and there is a skittle alley. At the time of writing it has been recently saved from closure, with a new owner and under new management. Delighted to say no changes to this fabulous pub are envisaged. The pub is one of the few remaining with no bar counter, selling traditional cider and real ale. It does not sell food as such, but a very hearty sandwich can be produced on demand and time permitting. Camping available – www.tuckersgraveinn.co.uk.

George & Pilgrims Hotel, 1 High Street, Glastonbury, BA6 9DP. 01458 831146 – Built in the late fifteenth century to accommodate visitors to Glastonbury Abbey and designated as a Grade I listed building, this is the oldest purpose-built public house in the south-west of England. Originally the Pilgrims' Inn of Glastonbury Abbey, but by the mid-nineteenth century the building was known as the George Hotel. Hence the current name. The front of the three-storey building is divided into three tiers of panels with traceried heads. Above these are three carved panels bearing the coats of arms of the abbey and of King Edward IV.

The Talbot Inn, Selwood Street, Mells, BA11 3PN. 01373 812 254 – A lovely old traditional coaching inn located in the heart of the historic village of Mells. This multi-room pub features a main bar situated in the main building with a 'sitting room' in the adjoining old barn. Look out for the superb old courtyard. Classic pub food is served in the main dining room, while snacks are served in the bar. In summer the 'Grill Room', across the courtyard, is open. There is a lovely walled garden to the left of the main building and upstairs there are eight upmarket bedrooms – www.talbotinn.com.

The George, High Street, Norton St Phillip, BA2 7LH. 01373 834 224 – Arguably one of the most famous pubs in the country dating from at least 1327, The George, therefore, has a good claim to be the oldest. The beamed bar features a distinctive fireplace. There are several other rooms used for drinking and dining, including a large dining room at the rear and a Dungeon bar, both accessed from the attractive cobbled courtyard. Steps lead from the car park to an enclosed garden which has views across the mead to the church. Now owned by Wadworth – www.georgeinnnsp.co.uk.

Cannard's Grave, Cannards Grave Road, Shepton Mallet, BA4 4LY. 01749 347 708 – The pub is located on the southern edge of Shepton Mallet and now sadly renamed 'Cannards Well Hotel'. Local legend (of which there are several versions) says that in the seventeenth century, the publican of the local inn, Giles Cannard (possibly also known as Tom the Taverner), engaged in criminal activity such as robbing, or aiding and abetting the robbery of, his guests, theft, smuggling and possibly forgery. His activities having been discovered, he either committed suicide or was convicted and hanged from the gibbet at the adjacent crossroads and buried nearby. Other explanations of the name include a tale that Kenred, a pagan and uncle of King Ine, who converted to Christianity was buried there. Perhaps the most likely story is that a thief convicted of sheep stealing was tried and hanged at the site. Now a modern hotel/pub with a restaurant and a well-stocked bar with 10 plus ciders including bottles and two changing guest ale – http://canardshotel.org.uk/contact.html

The City Arms, 69 High Street, Wells, BA5 2AG. 01749 677 768 – In 1810 the City of Wells jail was closed and later became the City Arms. The main bar retains the small barred windows and low-vaulted ceilings of its former existence. The building encloses a courtyard on three sides, with outdoor seating. There is extensive food service in the bar, bistro and restaurant, made to order using fresh local produce.

The Full Moon, 42 Southover, Wells, BA5 1UH. 01749 675 592 – A smart, friendly locals' free house just off the city centre. The interior of the pub comprises a public bar with sports TV and jukebox and a quieter lounge area, which is divided between the bar and a snug-like area. Out back is the city's largest pub courtyard and a beer garden beyond. Thatcher's Traditional cider is served. Family and dog friendly.

Cross Keys, 20 High Street, Rode, BA11 6NZ. 01373 830 900 – Reopened in 2004 after over ten years of closure, this was originally the brewery tap for the long-closed Fussell's brewery and, more latterly, a Bass depot. Sympathetically restored, it has succeeded in bringing back a strong village trade. Owned by the Butcombe Brewery. A passageway, featuring a deep well, links the two bars. There is also a large restaurant. Look out for the fascinating clock mechanism in the restaurant. There are three camp sites within a couple of miles: Burrow Farm (on way to the Mill pub) being the nearest, then Lower Chatley Farm at Woolverton and Vagg's Hill Farm (on a minor road to Farleigh Hungerford). The range of buildings opposite once formed one building, possibly the market hall. The roof timbers are original throughout and have been dated to 1428 – www.thecrosskeysrode.co.uk.

CHAPTER 6

Bath & North East Somerset

We begin this section at its southernmost point, **Midsomer Norton**. 'Norton' means 'north enclosure', from the Old English, although the use of Midsomer to distinguish it from other 'Nortons' seems to be of later origin and not mentioned until 1334. The main point of interest here is the **Midsomer Norton Railway Museum** (www.sdjr.co.uk) in Silver Street. This museum, naturally enough based at the town's railway station, includes restored station buildings, a signal box and goods shed. The museum is in

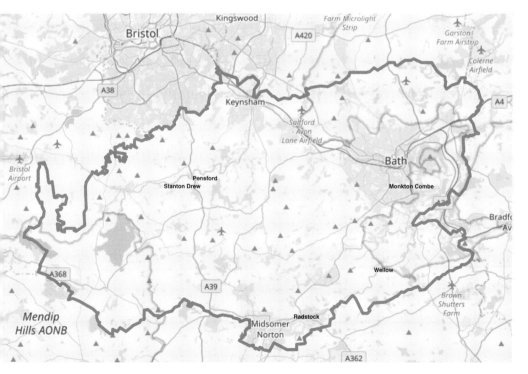

Map of Bath & North East Somerset. (BANES)

an old stable block. It has almost a quarter of a mile of railway line and a diesel locomotive.

Next up is **Radstock**. The town has been settled since the Iron Age, but its importance grew after the construction of the Fosse Way, a Roman road. The growth of the town occurred after 1763, when coal was discovered in the area. Large numbers of mines opened during the nineteenth century, including several owned by the Waldegrave family, who had been Lords of the Manor since the English Civil War. Admiral Lord Radstock, brother of George, fourth Earl Waldegrave, took the town's name as his title when created a baron.

Radstock is home to the **Radstock Museum** (www.radstockmuseum.co.uk) which is housed in a former market hall, and has a range of exhibits that offer an insight into north-east Somerset life since the nineteenth century. Many of the numerous exhibits relate to local geology and the now disused Somerset coalfield. When the last mine in the Somerset coalfield closed in 1973 a group of local people wanted to recognise the work of the Somerset miners and the result is an extensive collection of artefacts from the area's coal mining history.

The museum is housed in the restored 1897 Old Market Hall and has galleries on two floors with exhibits relating to blacksmithing, coalmining, shoe and boot making, printing and local breweries, along with a reconstructed coalmine and a Victorian street. Other displays include fossils, geology, agriculture and local railways with artefacts from the Somerset Coal Canal, Somerset and Dorset and Great Western Railways and a Victorian classroom. There is an admission charge.

The town of Radstock is also home to **Writhlington School**, famous for its orchid collection, and a range of educational, religious and cultural buildings and sporting clubs. The spoil heap of Writhlington colliery is now the Writhlington Site of Special Scientific Interest, which includes 3,000 tons of Upper Carboniferous spoil from which more than 1,400 insect fossil specimens have been recovered. The complex geology and narrow seams made coal extraction difficult. Tonnage increased throughout the nineteenth century, reaching a peak around 1901, when there were seventy-nine separate collieries and annual production was at 1.25 million tons per annum. However, due to local geological difficulties and manpower shortages, output declined and the number of pits reduced from thirty at the beginning of the twentieth century, to just fourteen by the mid-thirties; the last two – Kilmersdon and Writhlington – closed in September 1973.

The Great Western Railway and the Somerset & Dorset Railway both established stations and marshalling yards within the town. The last passenger train services to Radstock closed in 1966. Manufacturing industries such as printing, binding and packaging provide some local employment, but in recent years Radstock has increasingly become a commuter town for nearby Bristol and Bath.

The Rev. John Skinner & Pioneer Archaeologists

One of the country's earliest archaeologists and antiquarians was the Reverend John Skinner, who was born at Calverton just east of Bath in 1772. He trained initially for the law but became vicar of Camerton, a calling to which he seemed particularly unsuited. Despite his pleasant countenance in the portrait overleaf, he possessed a 'quarrelsome nature' and was quick to incur the dislike of his congregation. Nonetheless, he became friends with Richard Colt-Hoare of Stourhead, escaping from his professional life into a love of history and local antiquities. Sadly, he did not follow best practice in this either. His preferred method was to employ some local miners to whack a hole through the top of a prehistoric barrow and send for him once they had done so. Even at this he seemed to find something to argue about:

On settling with the 4 labourers at Priddy, I was much displeased with their imposition: they had, during Wednesday, Thursday and Friday, it is true, opened 15 barrows (!!), that is they had dug holes into them: but many required to be sunk three feet deeper to come to the interment, which we had no time to bestow; and yet they were dissatisfied with £2/14/6d I bestowed on them in money and food for their work, but I was determined to give them no more, as I am sure they must have idled away their time, and not done above half a day's work each.

The Rev. John Skinner. (Radstock Museum).

He was fascinated by the Neolithic burial mounds that he came across throughout the area and dug into as many as he could. His excavations were very much of their time, but unlike many contemporaries his thirst was for knowledge and understanding rather than the mere collection of bones or pots. In his journal of 1824, he divides the prehistoric into 'three epochs' and was one of the first people to recognise that different toolmaking materials belonged to different ages and outlined a system of categorisation that is still used today.

> 1, namely before the discovery of the metals, 2, after the use of edged tools became general, 3, when mankind had arrived at the highest pitch of perfection in their adornments – in other words I propose arranging the indicia of the savage inhabitants of this country. The truth of this position when applied to the subject under our consideration: – by their works shall ye know them.

Skinner's barrow diggings in North Somerset lasted from 1815 until 1832 and included Stoney Littleton as well as the massacre at Priddy. His journals number over a hundred thick volumes, and he wrote and sketched almost every day; his handwriting was so poor that he had his brother transcribe them before binding them into books for him. They were left to the British Museum upon his death locked in iron chests not to be read until fifty years later, though he later changed his mind on this. They are now in the British Library, unpublished and largely unexamined.

A difficult man, at odds with the world, greatly saddened by the deaths of most of his family and exhausted by his arguments with parishioners and gentry alike, in October 1839 he took his gun into a local wood and blew his brains out. One year later all his furniture and effects were auctioned off at the rectory and it must be assumed that any of his collections not previously donated were lost. It is probably down to his cantankerous personality and mode of exit that his work was not more highly valued in the past.

By the middle of the nineteenth century barrow-digging was becoming more than a gentlemanly pursuit and it was realised that better records and a more scientific approach was needed. Dr John Thurnam was a surgeon who moved to Wiltshire in 1851 and saw excavation as a means of advancing medical knowledge by studying its skeletons and skull shapes. It was Thurnam who carried out the first excavations at West Kennet, apparently using his patients as his labour force. Luckily, he missed most of its bone-filled chambers and their thirty-six or so inhabitants which enabled them to be more skilfully examined by Stuart Piggott in the mid-1950s.

The man who truly set archaeology apart as a science and laid foundations which are still followed today was the gloriously named Lieutenant-General Augustus Henry Lane Fox Pitt-Rivers. He was not involved locally, but after inheriting large estates at Cranborne Chase in Dorset he devoted the years 1880 until his death in 1900 to the meticulous excavation and recording of the prehistoric remains on his estate, carefully recording and publishing the results himself and setting the benchmark for those that followed.

Heading from Radstock towards Bath is the picturesque village of **Wellow** (www.wellowparish.info), and near there is **Stoney Littleton Long Barrow** (www.english-heritage.org.uk/visit/places/stoney-littleton-long-barrow). This is a Neolithic chambered tomb with multiple burial chambers measuring almost 100ft in length and 50ft wide at the south-east end.

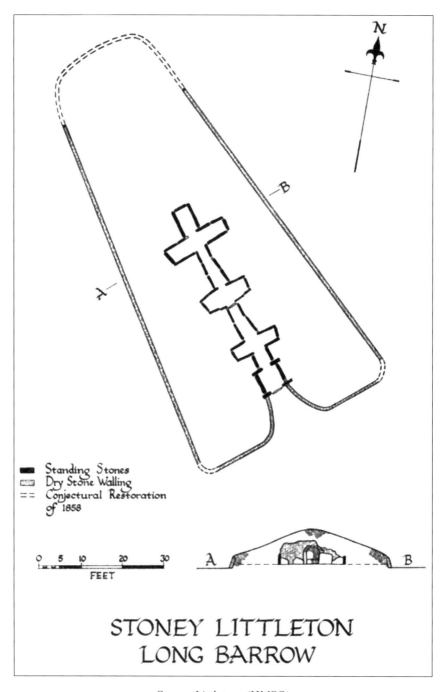

STONEY LITTLETON
LONG BARROW

Stoney Littleton. (HMSO)

It stands nearly 10ft high and consists of a 42ft long gallery with three pairs of side chambers and an end chamber. There is a fossil ammonite decorating the left-hand door jamb. The site was excavated by John Skinner around 1816, who gained the entry through a hole originally made by a local farmer looking for stone to repair his roads, in about 1760. The excavation revealed the bones (some of which were burnt) of several individuals.

In Wellow itself, and a minor point of interest, is the village's **Railway Station**. This was on the Somerset and Dorset Joint Railway line. The station opened in 1874 and closed in 1966. The station building was converted into a house by the pop artist Peter Blake and his then wife Jann Haworth in the mid-1970s, during their Brotherhood of Ruralists period. The signal box at the northern end of the down platform has also been converted for residential use. The station's canopy is still visible from nearby green space where the rail track ran south of the station. The house sports a weather vane with a steam engine finial.

On the outskirts of Bath, near Monkton Combe, is **Dundas Aqueduct**, (www.canalrivertrust.org.uk/places-to-visit/dundas-aqueduct) which carries the Kennet and Avon Canal over the River Avon and the Wessex mainline railway from Bath to Westbury. It was built by John Rennie and chief engineer John Thomas between 1797 and 1805, and James McIlquham was appointed contractor. It is named after Charles Dundas, the first chairman of the Kennet and Avon Canal Company. The aqueduct is 150 yards long with three arches built of Bath Stone, Doric pilasters, and balustrades at each end. The central semi-circular arch spans 64ft, while the two oval side arches span 20ft. Also within the area is the **Claverton Pumping Station,** (www.claverton.org) located in Ferry Lane, Claverton. This is a water pumping station with a waterwheel that pumps water from the River Avon to the Kennet and Avon Canal using power from the flow of the River Avon. It has been designated as a Grade II listed building, a rare surviving example of the technology of the late Georgian period; the pump started work in 1813, the year *Pride and Prejudice* was published. This amazing feat of engineering uses the power of the River Avon to lift water up 48ft into the Kennet and Avon Canal above. Burning no fuel and making no waste, it is the ultimate in environmentally friendly technology.

On the southern slope of Bath is **Culverhay Castle** at Englishcombe. To the east of the village church, the ringwork design is up to 5ft deep in places. During the first half of the thirteenth century, a stone circular keep and low curtain wall were built at the castle, along with one or two other stone buildings within the ringwork. A medieval deer park may have been attached to the castle. Estimates of the date of the original building range from the late eleventh to the early thirteenth century. The castle site was excavated by archaeologist Nigel Pounds in 1938.

We now enter the **City of Bath** (www.visitbath.co.uk) proper. It is fair to say its reputation rests on two things: the **Roman Baths** (www.romanbaths. co.uk) and its Georgian Architecture (www.museumofbatharchitecture.org. uk). It has been a World Heritage Site since 1987, which is a landmark or area selected by UNESCO (the United Nations Educational, Scientific and Cultural Organization) as having cultural, historical, scientific or other form of significance, and is legally protected by international treaties. The sites are judged important to the collective interests of humanity. Bath is the only city within the United Kingdom designated as such.

Legend has it that the city was founded by King Bladud who, having contracted leprosy and been banished into exile, found employment as a swineherd. One day, he noticed several of his pigs rolling around in mud. Those that did, subsequently suffered no skin diseases, unlike those who had not partaken of the mud bath. Next, Bladud immersed himself in it and was cured of his leprosy. This incident is supposed to have occurred at the village of Swainswick, around two miles from the later site on which the city was founded.

Local folklore also has it Bladud later died while trying to fly off **Solsbury Hill** using a pair of homemade wings. If true, then two public houses in the lower vicinity of the village, the Bladud Arms and the Bladud Head, located at the top and bottom of a hill respectively, attest to the fact that on landing he fell facing forward. True or not, only the Head remains as a current hostelry. Although Peter Gabriel made Solsbury Hill famous in his 1977 hit, locals will always correct strangers that its real name is Little Solsbury Hill. Whatever one chooses to call it, the site was an Iron Age hill fort occupied between 300 BC and 100 BC, comprising a triangular area enclosed by a single univallate rampart, faced inside and out with well-built dry stone walls and infilled with rubble. The rampart was 20ft wide and the outer face was at least 12ft high. The top of the hill was cleared down to the bedrock, then substantial huts were built with wattle and daub on a timber frame. After a period of occupation, some of the huts were burned down, the rampart was overthrown, and the site was abandoned, never to be reoccupied. This event is probably part of the Belgic invasion of Britain in the early part of the first century BC. The hill is near the Fosse Way Roman Road as it descends Bannerdown hill into Batheaston on its way to Bath. The site is a possible location of the Battle of Badon, fought between the Ancient Britons (under the legendary King Arthur) and the Saxons and the hilltop shows the remains of a medieval or post-medieval field system. The hill also has two disused quarries, one listed on the north-west side on a 1911 map, and another one listed between 1885 and 1900 as an old quarry on the west side. It was acquired by the National Trust in 1930.

Despite these historic landmarks, Bath is, of course, more closely associated with another set of occupants: the Romans. They called the city Aquae Sulis, and probably began building a formal temple complex sometime around the AD 60s. The Romans had, no doubt, arrived in the area shortly after their arrival in Britain in AD 43 and there is evidence that their military road, the Fosse Way, crossed the river Avon at Bath. An early Roman military presence has been found just to the north-east of the bath complex in the Walcot area of modern Bath. Not far from the crossing point of their road, they would have been attracted by the large natural hot spring which had been a shrine of the Celtic Brythons, dedicated to their goddess, Sulis. This spring is of natural mineral water and is the only spring in Britain officially designated as 'hot'. The name is Latin for 'the waters of Sulis'. The Romans identified the goddess with their own goddess Minerva, and encouraged her worship. The similarities between Minerva and Sulis helped the Celts adapt to Roman culture. The spring was built up into a major Roman Baths complex associated with an adjoining temple. About 130 messages to Sulis scratched onto lead curse tablets (*defixiones*) have been recovered from the Sacred Spring by archaeologists. Most of them were written in Latin, although one discovered was in Brythonic, and usually laid curses upon those whom the writer felt had done them wrong. This collection is the most important found in Britain.

The **Roman Baths** complex is a major tourist attraction and together with the **Pump Room** (www.thepumproombath.co.uk), receives more than a million visitors a year. The Roman Baths themselves are below the modern street level. There are four main features: the Sacred Spring, the Roman Temple, the Roman Bath House and the museum, which holds finds from Roman Bath. The buildings above street level date from the nineteenth century. Visitors can tour the baths and museum but cannot enter the water.

At the very beginning of the eighteenth-century Queen Anne visited the city on two occasions to 'take the waters', and with this royal seal of approval, she was followed by society's elite. In their wake came the middle classes. In fact, the city became so popular it quickly became apparent that the medieval accommodation was no longer fit for purpose and so a programme of building – the like rarely seen anywhere in the world – commenced, and within a few decades Bath had become one of Europe's greatest architectural triumphs. The crowning jewels are the **Royal Crescent** and **King's Circus**, but there are many, many other architectural landmarks and sites worth investigating.

John Wood the Elder and his son, the Younger, are the two architects most associated with this magnificent achievement. Most of the buildings are of Bath Stone, which gives the distinctive 'honey' look, and was quarried by Ralph Allen from his nearby Combe Down mines. He commissioned the building of **Prior Park**, situated on a hill overlooking the city, to showcase the properties of this stone as a building material. The house, listed Grade I, is now used by Prior Park College, while the surrounding parkland is owned by the National Trust. Allen was also responsible for **Sham Castle**, a folly situated on Claverton Down that is really just a wall meant to look like the entrance to a grand medieval fortress. The 'castle' is a Grade II listed building and was built to 'improve the prospect' from Allen's town house, in the middle of the city.

In the eighteenth and early nineteenth centuries Bath was the most fashionable place outside London and many people stayed in the city for the 'season' (which ran between October and May). As well as these, many famous people visited or stayed in Bath for shorter times. And these are commemorated by plaques attached to the front of the places they stayed (www.bath-heritage.co.uk/map) which included William Wordsworth, Admiral Nelson, Charles Dickens, Gainsborough, Sheridan, Livingstone and William Wilberforce.

To learn more about the history of the city, there are numerous museums to visit. The **Museum of Bath Architecture** – formerly the Building of Bath Museum and the Building of Bath Collection – (www.museumofbatharchitecture.org.uk) which occupies the Countess of Huntingdon's Chapel and provides exhibits that explain the building of the Georgian-era city. Other museums include **The Museum of Bath at Work** (www.bath-at-work.org.uk), based on a former tennis court dating from 1777, which contains a series of authentically reconstructed workplaces, workshops and display galleries that bring back to life 2,000 years of the city's working life, and the **Holburne Museum** (www.holburne.org) located in Sydney Pleasure Gardens. The city's first public art gallery, the Grade I listed building is home to fine and decorative arts built around the collection of Sir William Holburne. Artists within the collection include Gainsborough, Guardi, Stubbs, Ramsay and Zoffany. The museum reopened in May 2011 after restoration and an extension designed by Eric Parry Architects, supported by the Heritage Lottery Fund.

Elsewhere in the city, at 19 New King Street, is the **Herschel Museum of Astronomy** (www.herschelmuseum.org.uk). Inaugurated in 1981, the museum is located in a preserved townhouse that was formerly the home of William Herschel and his sister Caroline. The modest townhouse covers five floors and includes two reception rooms on the ground and first floor. It was from this house that Herschel discovered the planet Uranus in 1781. The building has been designated a Grade II listed building and was restored in 1981 and again in 2000, using period detailed wallpaper based on fragments discovered in other Bath houses, and carpets based on eighteenth-century designs.

Jane Austen and Bath

The connection between the city of Bath and the author of English Literature classics such as *Pride & Prejudice*, *Sense & Sensibility* and *Emma* stretches back before her birth in 1775. In 1764, Jane Austen's parents were married in the city (at St Swithin's Church, Walcot) before leaving for Steventon, where Jane's father, George Austen, was rector. And then, while Jane was growing up, relatives on her mother's side were constant visitors to the city, to the point where they rented a permanent residency (at No.1 The Paragon). The relatives had family to stay over the years and we know that Jane stayed with them near the end of 1797. She was back in Bath two years later, but this time stayed at an address in Queen Square. Between these visits, she began the novel that would eventually become *Northanger Abbey*, which is set in the city.

At the end of 1800 her father retired and announced the intention to move the family to Bath. For most of the time they lived in Bath, it was at No.4 Sydney Place, opposite Sydney Gardens. In late 1804, they moved to a house at Green Park Buildings East, but a couple of months later, Jane Austen's father suddenly died. He is buried at the church where he was married forty-one years earlier. With his death came financial difficulties and so the family (Jane, her sister and their mother) found themselves moving within the city – first to Gay Street and then Trim Street – before finally leaving the city for good in 1806.

Although it is said that Jane was happy to physically leave Bath, Bath never seems to have left her, as more than a decade after leaving, she wrote a love letter to the city in the form of *Persuasion*, set mainly in the city; it is one of the most romantic novels in the entire canon of English Literature.

Bath Abbey (www.bathabbey.org) in the heart of the city, is a former Benedictine monastery. It was founded in the seventh century but reorganised in the tenth and then rebuilt in the twelfth and sixteenth centuries; major restoration was also carried out in the 1860s. It is one of the largest examples of Perpendicular Gothic architecture in the West Country. The church is cruciform in plan and seats a congregation of 1,200. There is a heritage museum in the vaults, while the abbey itself is Grade I listed. Its west front includes sculptures of angels climbing to heaven on two stone ladders. Some of the figures are upside down, depicting fallen angels destined for the fiery pit.

Another place worth visiting within the city is the **Jane Austen Centre** (www.janeausten.co.uk) located in Gay Street. This is a permanent exhibition of the writer's time in the city, first as a visitor during the late eighteenth century, and then as a resident for the first six years of the nineteenth century. The building in which the centre is situated is itself designated a Grade II listed building. Among the exhibits is a life-size waxwork, unveiled at the centre in 2014. The centre also organises the world-famous **Jane Austen Festival** (www.janeaustenfestivalbath.co.uk) which takes place in the city every September.

During the English Civil War, the city was garrisoned for Charles I; £7,000 was spent on fortifications, but on the appearance of parliamentary forces the gates were thrown open and the city surrendered. It became a significant post for the New Model Army under William Waller. Bath was retaken by Royalists following the Battle of Lansdown, fought on the northern outskirts of the city on 5 July 1643.

Battle of Lansdown

By late May 1643, Lord Hopton's Royalist army had captured most of the south-west of England. Joined by the Earl of Hertford, he then advanced eastward into Parliamentarian-held territory. Sir William Waller's army held Bath, to obstruct their further advance. On 2 July 1643 the Royalists seized the bridge at Bradford-on-Avon. On 3 July, skirmishes took place at Claverton and at Waller's positions south and east of Bath. Waller retired to a strong position on Lansdown Hill, northwest of Bath while the main Royalist force moved north through Batheaston to Marshfield. Hopton's forces encountered this position on 4 July and were unpleasantly surprised at its strength. They withdrew five miles north east to Marshfield, while their rearguard repulsed an attempt by Waller's cavalry to pursue. Early on 5 July, Waller moved to the north end of Lansdown Hill, where he built crude breastworks for his infantry, and sent some of his cavalry against Hopton's outposts. They put to flight some badly led Royalist cavalry, and the alarm caused all of Hopton's army to form up and to begin advancing west until they came in sight of Waller's position. After indecisive skirmishing for two hours, Hopton again tried to withdraw.

Waller once again sent his horse and dragoons against the enemy rearguard, and this time they routed the Royalist cavalry, although the infantry stood firm. Hopton's army turned about and defeated the Roundhead cavalry in a confused action. With his Cornish foot regiments already advancing without orders, Hopton at last attacked Lansdown Hill. As they charged up the steep slopes towards the Parliamentarian position on the crest, Hopton's cavalry suffered badly, and many panicked. 1,400 of them fled, some as far as Oxford. Under Sir Bevil Grenville, Hopton's Cornish pike men stormed Waller's breastworks, while Royalist musketeers outflanked Waller through the woods on each side of his position. Grenville was mortally wounded in hand-to-hand combat as Parliamentarian horse counter-attacked and were driven off.

Waller's infantry fell back to a wall across the crest of the hill from where they kept up musket fire until dark fell. During the night, they withdrew silently, leaving burning matches on the wall to deceive the Royalists that they still held the position. The day after the battle, a Royalist ammunition cart exploded. Hopton was injured and temporarily blinded. The loss of the powder and the absence of most of their horses meant that the Royalists could not fight another action. Meanwhile, Waller had retired to Bath, where he had been reinforced and was ready to attack again. Hopton's army retreated in low spirits to Devizes. Hopton's army was in such a poor situation before their retreat that his military opponent, but old friend, Waller offered him hospitality in Bath, though he refused it. The site of the battle is marked by a monument to Sir Bevil Grenville, who died after the battle in Cold Ashton Rectory.

In April 1942, during the Second World War, the city of Bath endured two nights of intense bombing from the Luftwaffe, which is now known as the **Bath Blitz** (www.bathheritagewatchdog.org/bathblitz). Deemed a 'safe' city, it was practically defenceless against the onslaught unleashed upon it, supposedly as a retaliatory attack for the bombing of the historical German cities of Lubeck and Rostock. Along with other cities such as Exeter and Norwich, these bombings have become known as 'The Baedeker Raids', so called as the targets were chosen from the well-known German guidebook.

Sir Bevil Grenville's Monument at the place where he fell. © Stuart Logan (cc-by-sa/2.0)

As devastating as this was, and many buildings were destroyed, it is said 'The Sack of Bath' – a programme of demolition and redevelopment undertaken by the city council in the 1960s – caused more of Bath's architectural heritage to be destroyed than all of Hitler's planes. In the heart of the city, near Kingsmead Square, the old labour exchange still bears the scars of the blitz – several shrapnel and machine gun marks pockmark the exterior.

On the outskirts of Bath is the area known as Twerton. Although a shadow of its previous industrial existence, this suburb was at one time one of the big wool centres in the region. This included **Twerton Upper Mill**. In the eighteenth century, England reached a peak of wool production. Soon new machines would drive up the demand for cottons and other materials, but for now, wool was king. In mills across the country, machines started to replace paid jobs that local people had held for generations. This change didn't always happen peacefully. In December 1797, magistrates in Bath learned of a plan by unemployed wool workers to march to the Upper Wool Mill at Twerton, burn it down and murder its owner – Samuel Bamford. Bamford had introduced mechanised shearing machinery which had put many of these men out of work; 1,000 men were expected to make the march and the magistrates ordered a company of soldiers and dragoons to defend the mill. However, only around sixty men showed up, they were arrested and later released without charge.

Heading fully out of Bath now and towards Bristol, the large village of **Saltford** is soon reached. Its **Manor House** – built in the twelfth century – claims to be the oldest continuously occupied dwelling in England. Other historic buildings in the village include the Norman church, **St Mary's**, which also dates to the twelfth century. The tower dates to earlier Saxon times, but has been extensively repaired with the top 10ft added later. Both the Manor House and church are Grade II listed buildings, as is the eighteenth-century **Brass Mill**. The Mill, which is also listed as a Scheduled Ancient Monument, is situated on the banks of the River Avon. It is the only surviving building still with a furnace and working water wheel from a group of eighteenth-century mills making copper and brass goods in the Avon Valley. The mill is cared for by a dedicated group of volunteers who form the Saltford Brass Mill Project and carry out husbandry tasks within the building and research the fascinating history of the copper and brass industry.

The next stop on our route is **Keynsham.** The town is listed in the Domesday Book as 'Cainesham', which is believed to mean the home of Saint Keyne. The site of the town has been occupied since prehistoric times, and may have been the site of the Roman settlement of Trajectus. The remains of at least two Roman villas have been excavated, and an additional fifteen Roman buildings have been detected beneath the Keynsham Hams. During construction of the Durley Hill Cemetery in 1877, the remains of a grand Roman villa with over thirty rooms was discovered. However, construction of the cemetery went ahead, and most of the villa is now located beneath the Victorian cemetery and an adjacent road. The cemetery was expanded in 1922, and an archaeological dig was carried out ahead of the interments, leading to the excavation of seventeen rooms and the rescue of ten elaborate mosaics.

At the same time as the grand Roman villa was being excavated at Durley Hill Cemetery, a second smaller villa was discovered during the construction of Fry's Chocolate Factory. Two fine stone coffins were found, interred with the remains of a man and a woman. The villa and coffins were removed to a place near the gates of the factory grounds, and construction on the factory went ahead. Fry's built a museum in the grounds of the factory which for many years housed the Durley Hill mosaics, the coffins, and numerous other artefacts. In 2012, Taylor Wimpey, about to develop the factory site, made a detailed geophysical assessment of the area, and discovered the additional fifteen Roman buildings, which were centred around a Roman road beneath Keynsham Hams, with evidence of additional Roman buildings that had been disturbed by quarrying.

Keynsham developed into a medieval market town after Keynsham Abbey was founded around 1170. It is situated at the confluence of the River Chew and River Avon and was subject to serious flooding before the creation of Chew Valley Lake and river level controls at Keynsham Lock in 1727. The town played its part in the Civil War as the Roundheads saved it from the Cavaliers and also camped there for the night, using the pub now known as the Lock Keeper Inn as a guard post. During the Monmouth Rebellion of 1685 the town was the site of a battle between Royalist forces and the rebel Duke of Monmouth. Monmouth had intended to attack Bristol (the largest and most important city after London at that time). However, he heard the city had been occupied by Henry Somerset, 1st Duke of Beaufort. There were inconclusive skirmishes with a force of Life Guards commanded by Feversham and these gave the impression that there was a much larger Royalist force in the vicinity than there actually was. Several historians have speculated that if Monmouth had marched as quickly as possible for Bristol at this point, when it was only protected by the Gloucestershire militia, he would probably have been able to take the city and the outcome of the rebellion might have been very different. Once Bristol had been taken, more recruits would have been attracted to the rebellion and a later march on London would have been possible. Instead, Monmouth left his headquarters at Keynsham Abbey and marched eastwards.

Before entering Keynsham, Monmouth's rebel forces had encamped at **Pensford**. The village had been a cloth centre based on local wool trade between the fourteenth and sixteenth centuries, but later its main industry became coal. Pensford and the surrounding area formed a major part of the Somerset coalfield. Worth visiting here is the **Pensford Lock-Up**, an octagonal eighteenth-century village guardhouse. This is a Grade II listed building and a Scheduled Ancient Monument.

The final stop within this section is the **Stanton Drew Stone Circles And Cove** (www.english-heritage.org.uk/visit/places/stanton-drew-circles-and-cove) which stand just outside the village of Stanton Drew and are among the largest Neolithic monuments in the country. The date of construction is not known but is thought to be between 3000 and 2000 BC, which places it in the Late Neolithic to Early Bronze Age. The Great Circle was surrounded by a ditch, and at 371ft in diameter is the second largest stone circle in Britain, after Avebury. It is accompanied by smaller circles to the northeast and southwest. There is also a group of three stones, known as The Cove, in the garden of the local pub, The Druid's Arms. A short distance away is a single stone, known as Hautville's Quoit. Some of the stones are still vertical, but the majority are now recumbent, while some have disappeared altogether. The site has been studied since the antiquarian John Aubrey's visit in 1664, and in recent times geophysical surveys have

The Pensford Lock-Up. © Neil Owen (cc-by-sa/2.0)

The stones at Stanton Drew. © Sandy Gerrard (cc-by-sa/2.0)

confirmed the size of the circles and identified additional pits and features dating from 4000–3000 BC. A variety of myths and legends about the stone circles have been recorded, including one about dancers at a celebration who have been turned to stone for dancing on a Sunday.

Food and Drink

The Apple Tree, Shoscombe, BA2 8LS (two miles from Wellow). 01761 432263 – A family-run eighteenth-century free house, tucked away down narrow winding lanes, in the village of Shoscombe, just to the south of Peasedown. It is an ideal stop for users of local footpaths and cycle paths. Lovely views over the little valley from the pretty garden and the part-covered patio. Note that parking can be very difficult – www.appletree-inn.co.uk

Druid's Arms, Bromley Road, Stanton Drew, BS39 4EJ. 01275 332 230 – Allegedly haunted by Grace, who was run over by a carriage outside, this is a charming village pub named for the stone circles that still attract Druids on the solstices. There is one bar, a separate dining room and, behind the fireplace, additional seating. The garden has 'The Cove' part of the historic stone circles, as well as a children's climbing frame and pets' corner – www.thedruidsarms.co.uk

The Brew House, 14 James Street West, Bath, BA1 2BX. 01225 805 609 – The on-site micro-brewery, produces two regular beers, malty Gladiator (3.9%) and the hoppier, citrussy Emperor (4.4%) and rotating seasonal beers. There are usually five guest beers, sourced mainly from nearby micros. The bar also has a four-tap craft beer font serving artisan beers from both the UK and around the world. Through the main entrance is a large L-shaped bar. The James Street Brewery vessels can be seen, behind a glass frontage, to the rear of the bar opposite the main entrance. To the rear of the main bar area is a dining area with open kitchen, among whose features are a rotisserie and smoke house, and a very large garden and patio, which in the summer makes an excellent sun-trap and in winter is enclosed by a heated marquee. Upstairs is the Tank Room, where live TV sports can be seen, and which hosts quizzes, movie nights and comedy. This room, which has its own bar, can be hired as a function room – www.thebathbrewhouse.com

Saracen's Head, 42 Broad Street, Bath, BA1 5LP. 01225 426518 – According to a plaque in its vicinity, it is said to be the oldest pub in Bath. Built in 1713, on the site of a much older inn, the name of the pub originates from 'Saracens', who were the enemies faced by the Crusaders – www.greeneking-pubs.co.uk/pubs/somerset/saracens-head

Garrick's Head, 7-8 St John's Place, Saw Close, Bath, BA1 1ET. 01225 318 368 – A theatre pub for over 200 years, but originally the town house of Beau Nash, Bath's eighteenth-century Master of Ceremonies; this local is reputedly the most haunted pub in the city. Four guest ales, mostly from local or regional micros, include some rarities. Three or four ciders. Traditional food sourced from local ingredients is served lunchtimes and evenings. Tables outside are ideally placed for watching the world go by – www.garricksheadpub.com

The West Gate, 38 Westgate Street, Bath, BA1 1EL. 01225 461642 – Situated in the bustling centre, not 100 metres from the famous baths, the West Gate is a lively meeting place with the features of a large traditional pub: long, narrow and comfortably furnished, and occupying two floors. The pub itself has a long-recorded history, thought to date back to 1611. It was recorded as one of Bath's original coaching inns, then known as the Angel. Served alongside its usually interesting beer range are at least five traditional ciders. Cask Marque accredited. www. greeneking-pubs.co.uk/pubs/somerset/west-gate

The Raven, 6-7 Queen Street, Bath, BA1 1HE. 01225 425045 – A busy eighteenth-century free house in the heart of Bath, just off Queen Square. The four guest ales come from far and wide, and the two 'House Beers' are brewed exclusively by local brewery Blindmans. All are served in lined (or 'oversized') glasses to ensure you get a full pint. Meanwhile, real cider, sourced from local producers, is always available. Rather usefully the main bar and the quieter first-floor bar serve the same range of ales. Food-wise the Raven is famous for its sausages and 'Pieminister' pies and is one of the few pubs in Bath serving food on Sunday evening. Bath and Borders Pub of The Year 2018 – www.theravenofbath.co.uk

The Salamander, 3 John Street, Bath, BA1 2JL. 01225 428889 – You'll find The Salamander also just off Queen Square. The pub features a well-stocked bar with a fine range of locally brewed Bath Ales, wines, ciders and spirits, including an extensive gin selection, served on the ground floor. Cosy corners to sit and eat, and plenty more seating upstairs. The menu consists of traditional British classics such as fish and chips, kedgeree, toad in the hole, cider-cooked ham, egg and chips, alongside many more – www.salamanderbath.co.uk

CHAPTER 7

North Somerset

We now enter the final section – North Somerset – and the first point of interest on our route is **Blagdon Lake Pumping Station.** This is a Grade II listed building located within the village's Station Road. It includes scientific and environmental exhibits and displays as well as a room dedicated to the charity WaterAid. One of the two steam-driven beam engines can occasionally be seen working. Outside, there is a nature trail. In 1984, it was decided to preserve the two remaining engines and

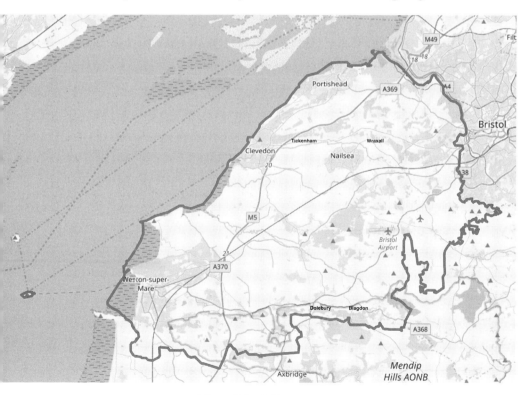

Map of North Somerset.

incorporate them as the central feature in the visitors' centre, including a museum in the old boiler house, which opened in 1988 and attracts over 30,000 visitors a year.

Close by is a cave at Burrington Combe – a limestone gorge near the village – called **Aveline's Hole** (www.discoveringblackdown.org. uk) which is the earliest scientifically dated cemetery in Britain. It dates from around 10,200 years ago and was discovered in 1797 by two men digging for a rabbit. Much of the collection has been lost, and although more than fifty individuals are represented, there are only two complete skeletons. Perforated animal teeth, red ochre and seven pieces of fossil ammonite suggest that some of the bodies were adorned. A series of inscribed crosses found on the wall of the Aveline's Hole cave are believed to date from the early Mesolithic period just after the Ice Age. The pattern is said to be comparable with others known from Northern France, Germany and Denmark. A gate has been installed in the cave to protect the engraving after consultations between English Heritage and other interested parties, including the landowner and English Nature. After the cave was rediscovered near the end of the eighteenth century, it was excavated and the entrance enlarged in 1860 by William Boyd Dawkins who named it after his mentor William Talbot Aveline. Access to the cave is controlled by the University of Bristol Spelæological Society and is restricted during the bat hibernation season.

Also close by is **Dolebury Warren** (also known as Dolebury Camp). This is one of the most important Iron Age hill forts in the county and lies near the villages of Churchill and Rowberrow. It is now a biological Site of Special Scientific Interest and a Scheduled Ancient Monument, owned by National Trust but managed by the Avon Wildlife Trust. Standing on a limestone ridge on the northern edge of the Mendip Hills, it was made into a hill fort during the Iron Age and was occupied into the Roman period. The extensive fort covers 22 acres (9.1 hectares) with single or double defensive ramparts around it. The name Dolebury Warren comes from its use during the medieval or post medieval periods as a rabbit warren, although the name Dolebury means 'the idol hill' from the Old English 'dwol' and 'beorg'. Various artefacts have been uncovered representing the long period of occupation of the site and these include

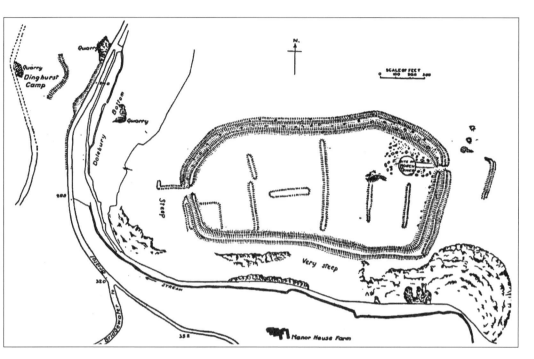

Earthworks at Dolebury Warren.

flint-work from the Palaeolithic era, bronze spearheads and pottery, along with Roman pottery and coins. There is also evidence of occupation during the Iron Age. The defences and Celtic field systems there date back to the seventh to the third century BC, though they might mask earlier developments. The hillfort was occupied until approximately 100 BC, though it is possible that it was reoccupied in the Roman and post-Roman periods. The archaeological consultant Peter Leach has suggested there may even have been a Roman temple built within the hillfort, while aerial photographs suggest the probable remains of an Iron Age or Roman coaxial field system. Local historian Robin Atthill also suggests that Dolebury may have re-emerged as an important centre of population in the fifth century.

In the medieval or post-medieval period, the remains of the hillfort were used as a rabbit warren to breed rabbits, providing valuable meat and fur. Many warrens were surrounded by banks or walls to prevent the rabbits from escaping; escaped rabbits caused damage to nearby farmland and meant a loss in profit. The warren at Dolebury is completely enclosed by the substantial ramparts of the Iron Age hill fort and thus provided an ideal location for this endeavour. The presence of pillow mounds and vermin traps demonstrate man's management of the site for husbandry. Ridge and furrow agriculture has been identified within the fort through aerial photographs. Some of these structures, along with earlier Iron Age features, have been damaged by subsequent quarrying. The site was visited by famous antiquarian John Leland in the sixteenth century. A three-storey building, believed to be the warrener's house and possibly a watch tower, surrounded by a garden, was in ruins by 1830. The site was visited in the early nineteenth century by John Skinner and surveyed in 1872 by Charles William Dymond. In 1906 the Mendip Lodge Estate, which included Dolebury Warren, was sold. It was first scheduled as an ancient monument in 1929. In 1935 Dolebury Camp was bought by Miss V. Wills of the W.D. & H.O. Wills tobacco company to prevent development. Dolebury Warren was notified as a Site of Special Scientific Interest in 1952.

Dolebury's Southern Ramparts © John Thorn (cc-by-sa/2.0)

The next stop on our journey has an incredible history. In 1811 **Weston-super-Mare** had fewer than 200 people living in this small fishing village, but within a century this had increased to the point that it was the second largest town in Somerset. This rapid expansion was due to the Victorian era boom in seaside holidays. The current population is more than 76,000. Its origins, however, go back as far as prehistoric times. The wooded promontory at the northern end of Weston bay was the site of a sizeable Iron Age settlement known as **Worlebury Camp**. In the first century AD, this was reputedly attacked and captured by the Romans with great loss of life, an event confirmed by recent excavations which revealed several skeletons showing the effects of sword damage. Worlebury Camp has been explored at various times since the mid-nineteenth century. From 1851 to 1852, Charles Dymond, Edwin Martin Atkins and Francis Warre excavated and surveyed it. Dymond returned in 1880 to continue the excavation, which lasted until 1881. Another century passed before the Woodspring Museum from Weston-super-Mare excavated more of Worlebury camp in 1987 to 1988.

Worlebury Camp.

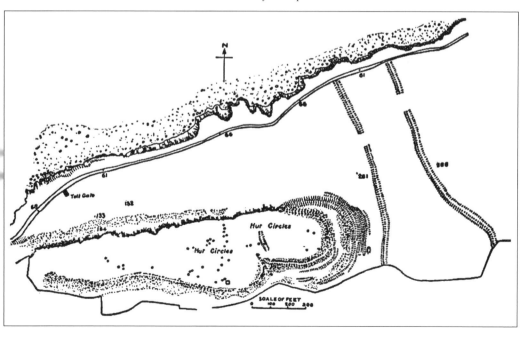

During the First World War, Weston-super-Mare played host to large numbers of soldiers who were billeted there for training. While there they learned how to dig trenches on the beach, and approaching 80 per cent of the trees in Weston Woods were chopped down for military purposes.

With so many men drafted into the army, women were recruited to take their jobs and the town had the honour of seeing the country's first woman tram driver, Beatrice Page. In 1914, Weston artist Alfred Leete's drawing of Lord Kitchener was used for the famous 'Your Country Needs You' recruitment poster. Meanwhile, during the Second World War, around 130 people were killed in bombing raids and over 1,000 injured, with large areas of the town destroyed.

Weston can also claim to have the only pier in the country which links the mainland to an island. **Birkbeck Pier** (www.birnbeck-pier.co.uk) juts out 1,150ft into the Bristol Channel – or rather it did. Despite being a Grade II listed building and on the Buildings at Risk Register, neglect and repeated storm damage has meant that it has been closed since 1994, during which time it has gone through many changes of ownership but remains derelict. The island which gives the pier its name was once home to Victorian refreshment rooms, a large concert hall, reading rooms, an extended pavilion, low-water jetty and the lifeboat station, now all sadly gone.

The collection at **Weston Museum** (www.westonmuseum.org) in Burlington Street includes archaeological exhibits, like those from Worlebury and there is a focus on local industries such as Royal Potteries, seaside holidays, costume and domestic life. There is also a replica of a nineteenth-century chemist shop, along with exhibits that explore life on the Home Front for the people of North Somerset during the Second World War, from air-raids to vegetable plots, as well as secret weapons developed on Birkbeck Island.

About three miles from Weston is **Woodspring Priory** at Kewstoke. This is a former Augustinian priory. It was founded in the early thirteenth-century and dedicated to Thomas Becket. It is a Grade I listed building owned by the Landmark Trust and rented out as holiday accommodation. There is also a small **museum** on the site with photographs and information about the history of the priory and its renovation by the

Woodspring Priory. © Roger Cornfoot (cc-by-sa/2.0)

Trust. The fifteenth-century barn, east cloister wall, farmhouse range, gatehouse, gates and mounting block, infirmary and west wall are also listed buildings.

There seems to be a plethora of hillforts in this section of Somerset and another one is **Cadbury Camp** (www.nationaltrust.org.uk/cadbury-camp) which is an Iron Age fort near the village of Tickenham. Although primarily thought of as an encampment from that period, from artefacts discovered at the site which include a bronze spear or axe head, it is likely that it was first used in the Bronze Age and still occupied through the Roman era into the Anglo-Saxon period. It was probably used by the Dobunni tribe and has been associated with Arthurian England and Camelot, but there is no evidence to support this. The 7-acre hill fort is well preserved and situated on a natural ridge between the Gordano Valley and the North Somerset Levels, next to Limebreach Wood, an ancient woodland and nature reserve. The Bronze Age spearhead is in the Museum of Somerset in Taunton.

Prehistoric Britain

Britain has been home to various species of human for almost a million years with the earliest traces yet discovered coming from Happisburgh on the Norfolk Coast. For long periods during that huge amount of time the land became uninhabitable as great ice sheets formed and drove people to warmer climates. The time before writing is known as prehistoric, and historians and archaeologists have found it useful to divide this vast period into loosely defined segments.

Palaeolithic: otherwise known as the Old Stone Age. During this period the British Isles were still joined to continental Europe, and this was the time of the classic 'cave man' wrapped in animal skins living in the mouths of caves, rough timber shelters and constantly on the move hunting animals and gathering roots and berries. It is a huge period and information is very sparse, consisting of a few flint tools and the odd bone, but the West Country scores are quite highly with remains found at Kent's Cavern in Torquay dated to about 43,000 years ago and evidence found in Gough's Cave at Cheddar (Chapter 3) to about 12,000 years ago.

The Mesolithic: when the ice age ended in around 10,000 BC, rising sea levels cut Britain off from continental Europe, but the land became occupied by a more sophisticated group of people who lived in large areas of what is now the North Sea. These hunter gatherers occupied a much more hospitable land, building some temporary settlements and refining their flint tools to catch deer, wild boar and fish. Again, the West Country was to their liking and their remains have been found on the Mendips and again at Gough's Cave (Chapter 3) where the famous Cheddar Man skeleton has been dated to 7150 BC.

The Neolithic c. 4,000–2000 BC: with this period, we are on much firmer ground, this was the time of the first farmers, the builders of the long barrows and causewayed camps. Recent evidence points towards there having been migrations of people and ideas from the Continent and beyond bringing with them the skills needed for farming and monument building.

This is the period that gave us Stoney Littleton (Chapter 6), the Sweet Track (Chapter 5) at Glastonbury, along with Stonehenge and Avebury.

The Bronze Age c. 2000–750 BC: the ability to refine metal which over the next thousand years replaced stone as the main material for tools and weapons arrived at Britain's shores during this period. Round barrows replaced long barrows and the land was divided up to look after animals and plant crops. The latest genetic research has shown that these people with their distinctive pottery known as beakers largely replaced the old Neolithic population by more than 90 per cent, but whether this was by conquest or simple migration is not yet known.

The Iron Age c.750 BC–AD 43: Ironworking techniques reached the country, again from the Continent, replacing bronze with a much harder and more plentiful material – iron. This innovation revolutionised life at home and in battle, high levels of art were achieved by the culture which became generally known as Celtic. The Celts were a highly organised and sophisticated group, far from the Roman propaganda of brainless savages. Their artistic and cultural development was rudely interrupted by the arrival of Romans and so ended the period of prehistory because, of course, the Romans introduced the written word.

The manor house of **Clevedon Court** (www.nationaltrust.org.uk/clevedon-court), up the coast from Cadbury Camp, dates from the early fourteenth century and contains many examples of Nailsea glass and a large collection of experimental pottery known as Elton Ware produced by Sir Edmund Elton in the late nineteenth century. The great hall and chapel block are the earliest surviving parts of the structure with the west wing being added around 1570, when the windows and decoration of the rest of the building were changed. Further construction and adaptation were undertaken in the eighteenth-century and the house was given to the National Trust in part-payment for death duties in 1960. The Elton family is still resident in the house, which is now open to the public, and the grounds include a selection of outbuildings, some of which date back to the thirteenth century.

Clevedon Court.

The coastal town of **Clevedon** itself (www.visitsomerset.co.uk/explore-somerset/clevedon), like its coastal neighbour Weston-super-Mare, became a fashionable seaside resort during the Victorian Age, although the lack of a railway terminus prevented the town from being overdeveloped. It has close links with both the poets Tennyson and Coleridge, the latter came here for his honeymoon in 1795 and stayed for two months in what has become known as **Coleridge Cottage** (www.britishlistedbuildings.co.uk/101129725-coleridge-cottage-clevedon) which is now a Grade II listed building and is situated on Old Church Road, as is **Tennyson House**, which is also Grade II listed. Alfred Tennyson had a close friend at Cambridge University called Arthur Hallam, whose mother was a member of the Elton family of Clevedon Court. Arthur, a poet and essayist, was engaged to marry Tennyson's sister Emily but died suddenly in Vienna in 1833 at the age of 22. His body was brought back to England and he was buried in the family vault at **St Andrew's Church** in Clevedon. In 1850 Tennyson wrote a poem, 'In Memorium', in tribute to his friend. In the same year he made his first visit to Clevedon. As well as the house named after him, a nearby road is called Tennyson Avenue. He was poet laureate between 1850 and 1892.

If you fancy a bit of a literary stroll, then **Poets' Walk** is a popular footpath which runs along the coast and around Wain's Hill and Church Hill at the southern end of Clevedon. The walk is said to have inspired both Tennyson and Coleridge, as well as William Makepeace Thackeray, who was a frequent visitor of the Elton Family. The formal path which exists today was constructed in 1929. Poets' Walk was designated as a Local Nature Reserve in 1993.

Back in town and in Old Church Road once more, is the **Curzon Cinema** (www.curzon.org.uk) This is one of the oldest continually running purpose-built cinemas in the world and is now owned by a community charity which continues to show the latest blockbusters. First opened on 20 April 1912, the Curzon is a fantastic slice of cinema history. As well as a 270-seat auditorium there is a smaller gallery room that can seat twenty-five.

Work to construct **Clevedon Pier** (www.clevedonpier.co.uk) began in 1867 and it has been described by Sir John Betjeman as 'the most beautiful pier in England'. The pier was constructed to attract tourists and provide a ferry port for rail passengers to South Wales; it is 1,024ft long and consists of eight spans supported by steel rails covered by wooden decking, with a pavilion on the pier head. Since its opening in 1869 it served as an embarkation point for paddle-steamer excursions for nearly 100 years. Two of the spans collapsed during stress testing in 1970 and demolition was proposed, but local fundraising and heritage grants allowed the pier to be dismantled for restoration and reassembled. It reopened in 1989, and ten years later was awarded the Pier of the Year from the National Piers Society, and a Civic Trust Award. The pier is a Grade I listed building.

Oakham Treasures (http://oakhamtreasures.co.uk) up the M5 from Clevedon, is located on Oakham Farm, Portbury Lane Portbury and is one of the largest privately owned museums of retail and farming history in the country. It opened in 2008 and has won awards for its collection of items which include an impressive display of vintage tractors and farm equipment.

Tyntesfield House (www.nationaltrust.org.uk/tyntesfield) near Wraxall is a Grade I listed building named after the Tynte baronets, who had owned estates in the area from about 1500. The site was formerly a sixteenth-century hunting lodge and was used as a farmhouse until the early nineteenth century. In the 1830s a Georgian mansion was built on the site, which was bought by English businessman William Gibbs, whose huge fortune came from guano (bird droppings) imported from Peru and used as fertilizer. By the 1860s Gibbs had become one of the richest men in England and had the house greatly expanded and redesigned. Much of the work was carried out by William Cubbit & Co., with designs by the architect John Gregory Case. A chapel was added in the 1870s and the family continued to own the house until the death of Richard Gibbs in 2001 by which time he had reduced his living quarters to just three rooms, with the rest of the house crammed full of possessions from the nineteenth century onwards. It is built largely of Bath Stone and includes a servants' wing, chapel, library, drawing room, billiard room and dining room. The house has been owned by the National Trust since 2002 and is a stunning example of the Gothic Revival style of architecture, new rooms are opened to the public as restoration is completed.

Tyntesfield House, Wraxall. © Brian (cc-by-sa/2.0)

To the east of Wraxall is the village of **Long Ashton.** Prehistoric and Roman artefacts have been found in the area, at the site of the Gatcombe Roman Settlement, but the village originated in Saxon times. The Domesday Book records it as *Estune* (the place by the ash tree). The manor house, **Ashton Court**, dates from 1265 and the country park attached to it has 850 acres of woodland and grassland surrounding it. Admission is free, and the house is the third most visited country park in England.

Near Wraxall is **Nailsea** (www.somersetguide.co.uk/Nailsea) and the town can lay claim to once having a hamlet within it called 'Nowhere'. Little is known of the area occupied by Nailsea before the coal-mining industry began, although it was used as a quarry in Roman times from which pennant sandstone was extracted. The Romans otherwise ignored Nailsea from AD 40–400 but left a small villa near Jacklands Bridge. Nailsea's early economy relied on coal mining, with the earliest recorded date for mining being 1507, when coal was transported to light fires at Yatton; by the late 1700s the town had many pits. Around this time Nailsea was visited by the social reformer Hannah More who founded a Sunday school for the workers.

The Elms Colliery (Middle Engine Pit), one of the most complete examples of an eighteenth-century colliery left in England is now in disrepair. It has been designated a Scheduled Ancient Monument and is included in the Heritage at Risk Register produced by English Heritage. Remains of the old pits, most of which had closed down by the late nineteenth century as mining capital migrated to the richer seams of South Wales, are still visible around the town. The coal mines attracted glass manufacturer John Robert Lucas, who established the Nailsea Glassworks in 1788 which became the fourth largest of its kind in the United Kingdom, mostly producing low-grade bottle glass. The works closed in 1873, but 'Nailsea' glass (mostly made by glassworkers at the end of their shift in Nailsea and at other glassworks) is still sought after by collectors around the world. The site of the glassworks has been covered by a Tesco supermarket car park, leaving it relatively accessible for future archaeological digs. Other parts of the site have been cleared and filled with sand to ensure that the remains of the glassworks are preserved. As for the historic hamlet of Nowhere, this was sadly demolished for development in 1967, although a small residential woodland, Nowhere Wood, is named after it.

The Middle of Nowhere © Sharon Loxton (cc-by-sa/2.0)

To the south-west of the town is **Nailsea Court**, now a Grade I listed building. This is the town's manor house dating from the fifteenth century. Eminent architectural scholar Nikolaus Pevsner described the house as 'historically highly instructive and interesting'. The exact date of construction is not known, but is believed to have been before 1574, when the initials of its then owner George Perceval were added to the chimney piece in the library. Perceval sold the estate to the Bristol merchant and member of parliament Richard Cole in 1582 and it was passed down to his descendants. In 1693, the house was purchased by Nathaniel Wade and around this time the roof was raised and a floor added into the original hall house. During the Monmouth Rebellion in 1685, Wade supported Monmouth; he was captured after the defeat of the rebels at the Battle of

Sedgemoor. Judge Jefferys condemned him to death at Taunton but King James, after having interviewed Wade, granted him a pardon. By the early twentieth century the house had fallen into disrepair, having been used for a long time as a farmhouse. Charles Edward Evans purchased Nailsea Court in 1906 and started a restoration programme which took seven years. He employed Arthur James Stratton, an expert on Tudor architecture, to reconstruct the west wing; the rebuilding also included the erection of a tower. The first version looked similar to a lighthouse and was changed to one of Tudor appearance which was incorporated into the south wing. The Whitefield family bought the house after Evans's death in 1944. They converted part of it into flats. The next sale was to a Mr McGrath in the 1970s and then a private development company purchased the house and grounds in the 1990s, after which it was converted into five private homes.

Nailsea Tithe Barn, at St Mary's Grove, is a restored tithe barn dating from 1480 and with adjacent **Holy Trinity Church** is part of Nailsea's historic heart. Having been used as a school for over 200 years, the tithe barn has now been fully restored to its medieval origins. As for the church, this dates from the fifteenth century and is now a Grade I listed building.

The Clifton Suspension Bridge (www.cliftonbridge.org.uk) spans the Avon Gorge and the River Avon, linking Clifton in Bristol to Leigh Woods in North Somerset. Since opening in 1864 it has been a toll bridge, the income from which provides funds for its maintenance. The bridge was built to a design by William Henry Barlow and John Hawkshaw, based on an earlier design by Isambard Kingdom Brunel. It is a Grade I listed building and forms part of the B3129 road. The idea of building a bridge across the Avon Gorge originated in 1753 and the original plans were for a stone bridge and later for a wrought-iron structure. In 1831, an attempt to build Brunel's design was halted by the Bristol riots, and the revised version of his designs was begun after his death and completed in 1864. Although similar in size, the bridge towers are not identical in design, the Clifton tower having side cut-outs, the Leigh tower more pointed arches atop a 110ft red sandstone-clad abutment. Roller-mounted 'saddles' at the top of each tower allow movement of the three independent wrought iron chains on each side when loads pass over the bridge. The bridge deck is suspended by 162 vertical wrought-iron rods in 81 matching pairs. The history of the competition to design and construct the bridge can be seen at the **Clifton Suspension Bridge Visitor's Centre** (www. cliftonbridge.org.uk/visit/visitor-centre) in Bridge Road on the Abbots Leigh side. The museum opened in 2015 and contains information about how the structure is maintained today. And by crossing this bridge from the Leigh Woods end, this takes us out of North Somerset and the end of our journey through the entire county.

Food and Drink

The Criterion, 45 Upper Church Rd, Weston-super-Mare, BS23 2DY. 07538 753 350 – Genuine free house and traditional community pub, just off the seafront in the Knightstone area. Believed to be one of the oldest pubs in town, it has interesting local photos on the walls. Pub games feature strongly, with darts and table skittles, plus a quiz on Tuesday. Bar snacks are available, with filled rolls at lunchtime. Between three and five guest beers are sold, with all beer styles and local breweries well supported.

The Waggon & Horses, 20 Old Street, Clevedon, BS21 6BY. 07428 793 430 – Once a coach house with horse and carriage yard to the rear. An unspoilt traditional community pub in the centre of Clevedon, with a public and a lounge bar, as well as a function room upstairs and a skittle alley. Pool, table skittles, cribbage and dominoes played, as well as petanque in the summer. There is disabled access to the rear, but phoning in advance is advised.

The Royal Oak, 43 High Street, Nailsea, BS48 1AS. 01275 853 127 – Set well back from the High Street, with its own large car park, this is a large one-bar community pub with several discreet drinking areas. The bar area has flagstone floors, and there is a mix of comfortable furniture throughout. There are patio tables at the front and a large rear garden that is very popular on summer lunchtimes. The pub supports skittles and darts teams, a Thursday quiz evening, live music on Saturday evenings and occasionally on Friday evenings. Guest ales may be reduced to one in winter – www.greeneking-pubs.co.uk/pubs/avon/royal-oak

Victoria Ale House, 2 Southleigh Road Clifton, Bristol, BS8 2BH. 01179 745 675 – Small and cosy nineteenth-century, Grade II listed Dawkins tavern, tucked away just off the bottom of Whiteladies Road next door to the Clifton Lido. Seven pumps offer beers from the Dawkins Brewery and changing guests, including from independent breweries. Often includes a dark beer. Two real ciders available. Two beer festivals are held annually, weekly quiz night on a Tuesday. Parking close by can be difficult.

Select Bibliography

Andrews, R. & Drew, K., *Rough Guide to Bath, Bristol & Somerset* Rough Guides 2012

Aston, Michael & Leech, Roger, *Historic Towns in Somerset* Somerset County Council 1977

Clarke, Jennifer, *Exploring the West Country: A Woman's Guide* Virago Press 1987

Crowden, James, *Literary Somerset* Flagon Press 2010

Davis, M & Lassman, D., *The Awful Killing of Sarah Watts* Pen & Sword True Crime 2018

Davis, M & Lassman, D., *Foul Deeds & Suspicious Deaths in & Around Frome* Pen & Sword 2018

Davis, M & Pitt, V., *Historic Inns of Frome* Akeman Press 2015

Dunning, R.W., *A History of Somerset* Somerset County Library 1987

Hawkins, Mac., *Somerset At War 1939–45* The Dovecote Press 1988

Hunt T.J. & Sellman, R.R., *Aspects of Somerset History* Somerset County Council 1973

Leach, Peter, *Roman Somerset* The Dovecote Press 2001

May, Andrew, *Bloody British History: Somerset* The History Press 2012

National Trust Handbook 2019

Newman, Paul, *Somerset Villages* Hale 1986

Sale, Richard, *Somerset* Landmark Publishing Ltd 2007

Tunstall, James, *Rambles About Bath & Its Neighbourhood 1876* Ulan Press 2012

Vesey, Barbara, (ed.) *The Hidden Places of Somerset* Travel Publications Ltd 2000

Whittock, Martyn, *Walking Somerset History* The Dovecote Press 1995

Wigfield, W. MacDonald, *The Monmouth Rebellion: A Social History* Moonraker Press 1980

Index